Mass Media, Consumerism and National Identity in Postwar Japan

Published in association with the Japan Research Centre at the School of Oriental and African Studies, University of London, UK.

SOAS Studies in Modern and Contemporary Japan features scholarly books on modern and contemporary Japan, showcasing new research monographs as well as translations of scholarship not previously available in English. Its goal is to ensure that current, high quality research on Japan, its history, politics and culture, is made available to an English speaking audience.

Published:

Women and Democracy in Cold War Japan, Jan Bardsley

Christianity and Imperialism in Modern Japan, Emily Anderson

The China Problem in Postwar Japan, Robert Hoppens

Media, Propaganda and Politics in 20th Century Japan, The Asahi Shimbun Company (translated by Barak Kushner)

Contemporary Sino-Japanese Relations on Screen, Griseldis Kirsch

Debating Otaku in Contemporary Japan, edited by Patrick W. Galbraith, Thiam Huat Kam and Björn-Ole Kamm

Politics and Power in 20th-Century Japan, Mikuriya Takashi and Nakamura Takafusa (translated by Timothy S. George)

Japanese Taiwan, edited by Andrew Morris

Japan's Postwar Military and Civil Society, Tomoyuki Sasaki

The History of Japanese Psychology, Brian J. McVeigh

Postwar Emigration to South America from Japan and the Ryukyu Islands, Pedro Iacobelli

The Uses of Literature in Modern Japan, Sari Kawana

Post-Fascist Japan, Laura Hein

Mass Media, Consumerism and National Identity in Postwar Japan, Martyn David Smith

Forthcoming:

Gathering for Tea in Modern Japan, Taka Oshikiri

Japan's Occupation of Java in the Second World War, Ethan Mark

Kenkoku University and the Experience of Pan-Asianism, Yuka Hiruma Kishida

Mass Media, Consumerism and National Identity in Postwar Japan

Martyn David Smith

THE ROYAL SOCIETY FOR ASIAN AFFAIRS

BLOOMSBURY ACADEMIC
LONDON • NEW YORK • OXFORD • NEW DELHI • SYDNEY

BLOOMSBURY ACADEMIC
Bloomsbury Publishing Plc
50 Bedford Square, London, WC1B 3DP, UK

BLOOMSBURY, BLOOMSBURY ACADEMIC and the Diana logo are
trademarks of Bloomsbury Publishing Plc

First published 2018

Cover design: Adriana Brioso
Cover image © Two little boys browse at a street bookstall in Hiroshima,
Honshu, Japan. (© John Chillingworth/Picture Post/Getty Images)

A catalogue record for this book is available from the British Library.

A catalog record for this book is available from the Library of Congress.

ISBN: HB: 978-1-3500-3078-7
ePDF: 978-1-3500-3077-0
eBook: 978-1-3500-3077-0

Typeset by Integra Software Services Pvt. Ltd.
Printed and bound in Great Britain

Contents

Acknowledgements

Many people have offered help, advice, support and critique over the years of the research project that forms the basis of this book. I want to thank friends and colleagues at the School of Oriental and African Studies for their support and criticism as the project developed, in particular Christopher Gerteis, Angus Lockyer, Lars Laamann, Andrea Janku and Mike Charney. The Japan Foundation provided a grant, which enabled me to spend time in Tokyo gathering the sources on which the book is based. Tokyo University of Foreign Studies gave me the opportunity to present parts of my research at several workshops, as did the German Institute of for Japanese Studies (DIJ) in Tokyo. Mathew Phillips kindly read and commented on numerous drafts throughout the entire project and provided much-needed friendship and support. Stefan Hubner read versions of different chapters and provided useful feedback and interesting insights. Torsten Weber at the DIJ in Tokyo also made suggestions and criticisms that helped to put the topic into a broader perspective. Thank you to Andrew Jackson for advice and friendship. Many thanks also to Phil Tomsovic.

Finally, thank you to Mari. Without her inspiration, love, support and patience this project would never have been started, and most certainly never finished. This book is dedicated to her, for giving me the chance to spend years reading, researching, writing and questioning, to my parents and grandparents who never had that chance and to Maiah and Masaki who put everything into perspective.

Introduction

Pleasure lies in wasting things, time, the body, money. I think waste is the best kind of accumulation. Me, I put as much effort in to waste as possible.
Ishihara Shintaro, *Heibon Punch*, May 1965[1]

In February 1952, in an interview published in the housewife's magazine *Fujin no Tomo*, Ichimada Hisato, the then governor of the Bank of Japan, pondered the different and challenging circumstances Japan found itself in as the US-led Occupation came to an end. A small, narrow country, economically inconvenient and not blessed with natural resources beyond an abundance of water, earning foreign currency would be central to Japan's future economic success. It would help to pay for the vital imports needed to continue trade, and also to improve the welfare of the people by providing capital for social and cultural projects. Hard work on the part of the Japanese people was essential, but by no means guaranteed. Japanese people were not efficient workers and an eight-hour working day was often equivalent to only two or three hours' work. In the business district of New York, one simply did not see people walking aimlessly around, 'documents are taken to the target desk via the shortest distance, quickly, looking only straight ahead'. In Tokyo, when office ladies carried documents around the office, they usually took the most circuitous route possible engaging in conversation with their fellow workers on the way. Creating a prosperous, independent country entailed putting peoples' time and energy to the most effective use. For the Japanese, this required a change in working culture.[2]

Former finance minister and chief negotiator for the San Francisco Peace Treaty Ikeda Hayato also used a New Year 1952 interview, in the popular daily newspaper *Asahi Shimbun*, to exhort the Japanese people to work harder to improve their living standards. Ikeda stressed that the best way to deal with

Japan's new economic and political situation was to get the people working together to cultivate an independent spirit. He somewhat mystically framed it as a dance, the tune for which 'does not come from the East, West, North or South, but from within'. Everybody danced in their own time, but life would get better if everyone pulled together.[3] Ikeda invoked a communal spirit, and like Ichimada he tied the individual to the nation in the quest for reconstruction of the country. Both statements had unsettling echoes of prewar and wartime calls for individual sacrifice in the name of national progress. Yet, in the early 1950s, the language of the war period was still in the process of being re-read and given new meaning within the postwar terms of peace and democracy.[4] In this context, the *Asahi* newspaper accompanied Ikeda's interview with a call for the government to be open with the people about the reality of the economic situation and to work to build a new lifestyle based on a nation of free individuals (*jiyū kokumin seikatsu*).

Even in 1952 life had certainly improved since the end of the war. The economy had returned to 80 per cent of prewar levels, and, although much of the benefit of this was concentrated in rural areas, there was no shortage of luxury goods and fine restaurants in fashionable areas of Tokyo, such as Ginza and Shinjuku. Still, in many cities, industrial workers, salarymen, teachers and intellectuals were still subsisting on salaries roughly one-third of prewar levels.[5] As economist Tsuru Shigeto wryly noted in *Fujin Kōron*, 'in reality we have chewing gum but no bananas, we have nylon stockings but no nappies'.[6] Nevertheless, the economic improvement that followed the end of the Occupation was rapid. In 1955, the Japanese economy stood at only 7 per cent of the American level, but by 1973 it had reached one-third. Within the space of two decades, the Japanese economy became the second largest in the world, and, by 1976, it accounted for around 10 per cent of the world's economic activity. The percentage of the workforce involved in farming fell from almost half in 1950 to 17 per cent by 1970, and large numbers of young people poured into the cities to work in the factories and expanding service industries, even as the cities expanded outwards making metropolitan lifestyles the 'defining experience of "modern" postwar society'.[7]

At the end of the Occupation, discussion and debate over the nature of nationalism and the meaning of nation was, together with class and humanity, intimately connected to the wider context of postwar reconstruction.[8]

A rapidly expanding popular media discussed and debated this national re-imagining and, over the period of high-speed economic growth, created a matrix of everyday life which connected individual Japanese to the story of national reconstruction and global reintegration. It began with the linking of the wartime rationalization movement to the goals of the US Occupation with the aim of bringing democratic freedoms to the Japanese people.[9] After 1945, wartime ideals of purity and purification turned to freedom and democracy. The purging of militarism and feudalism harnessed militaristic ideology, but 'universal "democratic" values now became the touchstone of purity'.[10] Yet, eventually, as Carol Gluck has noted, the emphasis on electoral politics and democratic freedoms in defining modern lifestyles was overwhelmed by the pursuit of the good life through consumption.[11] In this book I trace the evolving nature of nationalism and national identity in relation to this growing consumerism during the two decades from 1952 to 1972.

I argue that, rather than individual freedom and democracy being overwhelmed by the growth of consumer society, the Occupation goals of peace and democracy became subsumed within it. I do this by examining the way the good life, and the consumption that drove it, was presented, promoted, debated and discussed in the growing popular written media. The process of political, social and economic transformation in Japan throughout the 1950s and 1960s exposed the disintegration of what Andrew Barshay has called the 'hegemonic nation' of wartime.[12] It threw up ambiguities, contradictions and difficulties for the top-down or bottom-up re-creation of nationalism and national identity. The political concerns of the Occupation, driven by the desire to promote democratic values, prevent the emergence of an autocratic state and, eventually, to simply ensure the country did not turn communist, were gradually incorporated into the promotion of economic growth through consumption. This process brought about a transformation in the nature of nationalism and national identity.

Rather than the familiar story of the Japanese turning away from nationalism and national identity immediately after the war, embracing economic nationalism in the 1950s and then cultural nationalism in the 1970s and 1980s, I argue that the process is better understood by considering the changing ways that the promotion of consumerism allowed individuals to relate to and think about the nation. The importance of individual subjectivity in the promotion of a democratic spirit in postwar Japan became tied to the rebuilding of the economy within a global modernity increasingly marked by the individual's consumption of goods and the creation of positive tropes of waste and abundance. With the growth of the popular media, the divisions between elite discourse and the masses were broken down and the free individual placed at the centre of the process of re-imagining the nation.

Dismantling the nation

To better explain this it is necessary to go beyond the usual conception of the nation and nationalism as bounded, other-defined identities given shape and substance by historical events. Brought to the fore in ceremony, spectacle or the staging of tradition, the idea of nation in this context is very much focused on the state and the work of intellectuals and elites. Here, nationalism is the promotion of a certain conception of the boundedness of the nation and the commonalities perceived to lie at the base of it. Instead, in the postwar period, I argue that ideas of nation were not only encouraged and spread by imposing narratives that secured the interests of particular individuals or groups onto society. They were subtly woven into discussions that sought to effectively represent the individual experience of urban life in relation to the rapid transformation brought by economic growth.

What is important is that the national did not only become grounded in un-reflexive forms of 'common sense', as Tim Edensor argues; it also became connected to what Miyoshi Masao has termed the 'relentless consumerisation of individual subjectivity'.[13] The goal was to convince newspaper, magazine and journal readers that the discursive Japan and the objective Japan were, or at least could be, one and the same.[14] In postwar Japan, the rapid growth of the media was part of the promotion of consumer society, but it also transformed the parameters of daily life within which the nation came to be experienced by the Japanese people. These discursive parameters gradually took objective shape as the transformation of the country under high-speed economic growth created the spaces and places of consumption which could become a matrix against which the experience of this daily life played out.

In a recent discussion of the problems of the definition of nationalism and national identity in Japan, Robert Hoppens has noted that two conceptions exist: nationalism as identity and nationalism as discourse. Nationalism as group identification assumes various common attributes and interests. Nationalism as an effort to assert one's own definition of these attributes, however, suggests diversity, contention and competition.[15] It is my contention that the promotion of consumer society in the popular media deepened the prospects for diversity, difference and discussion in postwar Japan. As Hoppens points out, Michael Billig's notion of nationalism as 'a tradition of argument' helps us to better understand the ambiguous nature of the concept. Yet, this way of thinking about nationalism and national identity also needs to overcome the assumption that identification with the symbols of nation, such as Billig's unwaved flag, needs to be continually worked on to ensure the meaning remains consistent and understood.[16] I aim to show that the meanings given to nation and nationalism, the terms of the debate and discussion, 'the argument' in Billig's understanding, are being continually reshaped and re-imagined within any given historical context. Not always by the arbiters of political, social or cultural tastes. As Tim Edensor puts it in critiquing Anthony Smith's top-down theory of nationalism:

> Particularly in contemporary times, any identification of national cultures would have to include a range of ... cultural producers-pop stars, advertisers, tabloid hacks, marketers, fashion designers, film and television producers and sporting heroes – as well as a host of popular cultural practices including dancing, sports-spectatorship, common pastimes, holidaying and touring.[17]

In the 1950s and 1960s, individual subjectivity and national subjectivity were intimately linked to the notion of Japan as a 'free' country in the context of the Cold War in East Asia. The rejection of the Japanese state in the aftermath of defeat and the promotion of democracy and individual rights during the Occupation combined with the beginning of rapid economic growth and the shift in focus to an economy geared towards domestic consumption in the late 1950s. This served to merge national identity with individual subjectivity, because the Japanese media promoted individual consumption in the name of the recovery of the Japanese nation as a whole. The Cold War context of the promotion of consumption and consumer lifestyles was not limited to Japan and, as elsewhere, national identity emerged through the media in collective tropes that imagined 'Japan' and 'Japanese' in relation to the growth of this consumer society within a Cold War discourse that emphasized the freedom of choice these lifestyles offered to the individual.

In Japan, the process of rejecting the prewar nation and rehabilitating words like *Kokumin* (citizen), *Minzoku* (people) and *Aikokushin* (patriotism) was not simply one of intellectual debate over the meaning and usefulness of the terms.[18] As high-speed economic growth brought the rise of popular culture, national identity and nationalism (understood as the discourse on national identity) could come to be found in a huge cultural matrix of images, ideas, spaces, things and practices.[19] It is in explaining this transformation that I want to use the term 'national subjectivity' as a means to understand the individual experience (as framed by the printed sources) of the changing nature of ideas of Japan circulating in the media. I introduce this term in the hope of escaping from the determined and normative influence of the term 'national identity'. Because, while 'national identities' may capture the plurality of national tropes that I argue for, and Brian McVeigh's notion of nationalisms helps to foreground the complex nature of the concept, the term 'national subjectivity' better captures the individual autonomy involved in thinking about the national in everyday life. McVeigh's nationalisms may differ in terms of the arbiter of national culture, but they remain top-down, managed and apparently impermeable.[20]

In the postwar period, as Japan emerged as an economic and technological superpower, the domestic, national and global were complicatedly entangled with each other.[21] Because national identity and nationalism are constantly being re-imagined in changing local and global contexts through an ever-expanding range of resources, and as the consumer society of the 1950s and 1960s promoted the autonomous individual as the core of social, cultural and economic life, in the period of high-speed economic growth the development of the popular media needs to be taken into account. Benedict Anderson has argued that the nation is an imagined social and cultural community given substance in individual consciousness by the technological innovation of the printing press and the growth of the written media.[22] It is in this context that the importance of everyday life becomes apparent. The world imagined through the shared experience of reading monthly or weekly magazines is clearly rooted in everyday life. Sarah Frederick has noted that, in interwar Japan, the act of creating 'a community of readers' in the housewife magazines was also designed to create a national imaginary for their readers.[23] The development of a media industry was a major component of the expanding consumerism of the Taisho and early Showa period.[24] Newspapers, magazines, movies, radio, and records and the increasing numbers of readers, viewers and listening audiences they attracted all laid the groundwork for postwar consumer society and the media industry. They also began the process of incorporating the individual reader into the creation of the magazine.

Tracing the development of publishing in the 1950s and 1960s, the number of new publications which appeared is striking. Between 1954 and 1971, the total number of published magazines doubled, and the number of weekly magazines almost tripled. The number of magazines aimed at women doubled, as did 'general interest' magazines.[25] In the late 1950s, as economic growth began to accelerate, there was a boom in magazine publishing in Japan. Magazines became larger and more stylish as weekly magazines came to take up a larger share of the market. By 1958 around 8 million copies were being produced each week, amounting to around 35 million copies per month. In all, by 1960, 598 million copies of weeklies and 481 million copies of monthly magazines were being produced. Growing economic prosperity supported this rapid increase, and the appeal of these magazines to the public lay in their ability to move hand in hand with the 'fast changing contemporary society'.[26]

Consumption as a national goal

The magazine that carried Ichimada's comments was founded by Hani Motoko in the early twentieth century. *Fujin no Tomo* sought to transmit practical knowledge indispensable for the improvement of daily life and Hani worked to unite women's movements and state bureaucrats in a commitment to 'modernizing the mores of and habits of ordinary women'.[27] After the formation of the National Spiritual Mobilization Campaign in 1937, to fight against luxury, waste and the consumption of foreign goods, movements to 'improve lifestyles' took on an important role and reached out to rural communities as well as urban housewives.[28] The alliance between women's groups and the state deepened after surrender, as postwar women's groups worked with the bureaucracy on projects to improve daily life and promote political participation.[29] In the 1950s, Japanese corporations took up these ideas and, by the end of the decade, over fifty corporations had initiated programmes with similar goals as a means of delineating gender roles to achieve better productivity from their male employees.[30] The issue of food rationing and survival brought these groups into cooperation and conflict with the state, and housewives' associations played an important role in consumer advocacy in the early postwar period.[31]

The process of lifestyle improvement began to redefine the citizen and the consumer and gradually blurred the boundaries between the two. This process connected the Japanese to a global Cold War in which, as Matthew Hilton has demonstrated, the link between consumption and the state was tied in with the geopolitics of the late 1940s and early 1950s. Throughout the 1950s and the 1960s, state officials liaised with women's and housewives' organizations as politicians on both sides of the 'Iron Curtain' promised their people a better life. By the 1960s, consumer society was seen as the best means of achieving this.[32] In Japan, as elsewhere, providing for necessities in the early postwar period gradually gave way to creating affluence for all and, eventually, by the late 1950s and throughout the 1960s, consumer society was promoted as an end in itself rather than a specific means of improving lifestyles. Consuming became less about rationalization and more about personal transformation. The politics of rationalization and thrift promoted by the lifestyle improvement movement was about creating a shared morality and a communal consciousness during a time of hardship. The announcement of the consumer as king in 1960 shifted the focus to individual subjectivity and the promotion of waste and abundance.

Of course, postwar consumer society did not emerge from a historical vacuum. During the Taishō period, the expansion of Japan's economy, urbanization and the growth of the popular media created spaces and images of consumption for an emerging middle class.[33] Barbara Sato has shown how images of the 'modern woman' in the media presented a graphic illustration of the rise of consumerism in the 1920s that also reflected the changing role and status of women. The promise of a middle-class existence had been overdetermined in the Taisho and early Showa period. Yet, by the mid-1950s, the individual consumption and middle-class lifestyles promoted by the Japanese state finally came within the grasp of the average housewife.[34] Consumer goods and their use came not only to define the private lives and social roles of the Japanese people, but also to shape the representation of ideas of nation in the mass media. In this context, ideas of nation in postwar Japan became difficult to separate from consumer culture.

In their account of women and the media in Japan, Lise Skov and Brian Moeran see a crucial rupture in the early 1970s, a paradigm shift resulting from the 'diverse changes' of the 1960s, student riots, demonstrations against environmental pollution and the Osaka Expo in 1970, which 'together with the oil crisis in 1973, led to the restructuring of the Japanese economy'.[35] For this reason, they chart the development of consumerism and popular women's magazines from the 1970s onwards. Skov and Moeran see the main trend of the 1970s as 'marked by a rediscovery of tradition'. As Marilyn Ivy has argued, advertising turned this concept into a pervasive national mass phenomenon. In this context, the past, typified by the popularity of academic works by medieval historian Amino Yoshihiko, or the countryside through the successful 'Discover Japan' campaign, can be seen as a play on tradition by the Japanese media accompanied by the revitalization among thinking elites of *nihonjinron* (theories of Japaneseness) throughout the 1970s.[36] For Skov and Moeran, the *nihonjinron* discourse can be explained as the work of 'tradition-mongering neo-conservatives bent on re-establishing the norms of earlier industrial capitalism: discipline, authority, the work ethic and the traditional family'.[37]

For many scholars, Japan finally embraced consumerism with the consumption boom of the 1980s. Jordan Sand, discussing the New Breed (*Shinjinrui*) of young urban consumers in the 1980s and 1990s, has concluded that their ambivalence developed from a paradox of sensibilities. 'Young Japanese of the 1980s longed for something outside Japan's managed consumer society, yet they were captive to its fashions'. They sought the vernacular spaces of the city as an antidote to the ubiquitous exhortations to consume, and in response to the commodification of all aspects of youth culture.[38] Although not so constantly bombarded by advertising or targeted by surveys and lifestyle guides as their counterparts in the 1980s and 1990s, the youth of the 1950s and 1960s were no less plagued by ambivalence and ambiguity.[39] The New Breed sought out Tokyo's vernacular spaces while yearning for a nostalgic rural landscape, and the young people of the era of rapid economic growth looked to escape from the rural and create those vernacular spaces even as the nostalgic, rural landscape they left behind was filled with concrete. Photo spreads and discussions in magazines such as *Mainichi Graph* and *Asahi Graph*, and in magazines such as *Shūkan Heibon* and *Heibon Punch* (whose 1950s and 1960s readership consisted of young Japanese from all parts of the country), promoted and debated the growth of an increasingly self-conscious consumer culture.

In the popular media of the 1950s and 1960s, both democracy and consumption were in the process of becoming 'Japanese' as the transwar period gave way to the postwar and new defining social, political and economic patterns emerged. This book seeks to expose that ambivalence and trace the ambiguities inherent in the rise of consumer society in the period from the end of the Occupation in 1952 to the end of the 1960s. Of course, state-led economic development dominated plans and policies for economic and social recovery from the trauma of the war. The transformation of the cities and the depopulation of the countryside brought about social problems such as food, housing, pollution and congestion that would have to be dealt with at the level of the state. Nevertheless, precisely because ideas of nation based on rationalization appealed to everyday life, as the money spent on essentials declined and everyday life became more and more tied to consumption, national identity itself became commodified through the popular media. This process was in no way unique to Japan. The depoliticization of national consciousness in the postwar was a consequence of government policy, but the process was not controlled by the state. The role of the state and intellectuals in defining the parameters of everyday life in postwar Japan gave way to market forces, consumption and a booming popular culture—a process that resulted in ambiguity and cynicism more often than consensus and homogeneity.

The growth of the popular media aided the consumerization of identities, national and individual, and this was connected to the wider political, social and economic transformations of the period from 1952 to the beginning of the 1970s. For this reason, I use magazines aimed at housewives and magazines aimed at young people in addition to daily newspapers and high-brow journals. The use of these sources, and the layout of the book, reflects the broadening of the debate and the expansion of the possibilities for national subjectivity (that is, as outlined above, the individual's connection to the national). The journals and magazines chosen targeted different audiences; nevertheless they all participated in the creation of 'national space' during the period of high-speed economic growth, and by juxtaposing them it is possible to see the overlapping and conflicting nature of many of the ideas of nation that emerged.

On top of this, many magazines were read by several people and people from ostensibly different target audiences would have read, or even bought, magazines aimed at a different demographic. Middle-class businessmen did read magazines aimed at housewives as well as magazines aimed at young people such as *Heibon Punch*. Nevertheless, it is important to note that this book is not meant to be an exhaustive account of the development of the written media in this period, neither from the perspective of publishers, writers or readers. Rather, I seek to offer some insight into the ways in which the growth of the medium itself could create a matrix of images and ideas of nation that could make sense in the everyday lives of the Japanese people, and help us to understand the contradictions and ambiguities inherent in the postwar experience.

Chapterization

The first chapter addresses the connection of Cold War concerns to the promotion of a consumer-oriented economic system in Japan. The flourishing of consumer society and the rise of popular media in the Taisho and early Showa periods had been cut off by the privations of total war and total defeat. Although the rise of consumption had transwar origins, throughout the late 1940s and early 1950s most Japanese were not in a situation to spend freely. Nevertheless, as the economic growth spurred by the increase in production to support the Korean War shifted in the mid-1950s to promote consumption as the driving force for economic growth, the popular written media began to rapidly expand. By the late 1950s, the housewife and her salaryman husband were important targets. With the advent of high-speed economic growth, they were joined by young single Japanese with disposable incomes.

By 1960, increasing affluence and a burgeoning popular media began to merge consumerism with ideas of nation and individual subjectivity. Cold War concerns helped to bring about this change. The chapter will show how the debate over consumption in the mass media gradually came to reflect the issues of peace and democracy and Japan's importance in the promotion of Cold War–free world values. This made clear a shift in the boundaries of, and between, consumerism, ideas of nation and individual subjectivity. The chapter will give an overview of the political and economic concerns behind the promotion of consumption and outline the emergence of a media which responded to and promoted, but was nevertheless dependent on, it. Many intellectuals began to search for a new form of nationalism centred on 'free' individuals. This would be underpinned by a democratic spirit manifested in the everyday lifestyles and culture of the Japanese people. By the late 1950s, that everyday life was becoming centred on a growing consumerism that connected the individual to the rebuilding of the nation within the context of the global concerns of the Cold War. This both propelled and was driven by the rise of popular magazines.

Chapter 2 looks at the ways in which, in the years after the Occupation, the key terms 'democracy', 'peace' and 'culture' became incorporated into the discourse over nationalism and the nation. Peace and democracy would best be achieved by firmly embedding the concepts within the everyday culture of the Japanese people. The changes needed to prevent a return to the authoritarianism of wartime would be most effective, and best achieved, at the level of everyday life. Everyday life also appeared, to intellectuals, to offer protection from the vagaries and rivalries playing out in the Cold War. I begin with an outline of the intellectual debates over the meaning and nature of nation and nationalism as the Occupation came to an end. The ambiguous nature of the concepts involved and the national and international political issues informing the debates played out in media discussion of more mundane issues. The chapter will look at how debate and discussion over food, diet and nutrition fused the importance of reshaping individual subjectivity and democratic consciousness to the necessities of everyday life and, in doing so, helped to connect individual subjectivity to the discussion and debate over nation and national identity.

The third chapter tackles the marketing opportunities presented by a vibrant, youth-led consumer society, middle-class domesticity and engagement with the outside world. I examine the 'relentless consumerization of individual subjectivity' in the postwar period, as the purchasing of consumer goods came to encompass the happiness of human freedom. By the late 1950s, popular magazines showed their readers what they should be, what they should aspire to, and what they should and could consume. Along with the young men drafted into factories and sales departments to power the 'Japanese miracle', the aspirations and horizons of the young women who moved to the cities were transformed by the growth of the market for mass weekly and monthly magazines. Magazines were bought and then widely circulated. The nature of the medium itself relied on, and promoted, the idea of waste as a virtue, and the freedom to waste became essential to the Japanese promotion of consumer society. The everyday banality of consuming helped to erode the political binaries of the Cold War. Yet, by the time of the Tokyo Olympics, the apparent influx of all things foreign was being widely criticized. Much of this fear revealed the increasing visibility of the young working men, and particularly women, who consumed and populated the new urban spaces, as the earning power of this younger generation began, due to the rapid nature of economic growth, to overtake that of the more middle-class, white-collar salaryman. The presentation of national identity in the popular media was part of a global process of postwar reconstruction. Individual subjectivity could be found in the freedom to spend and to waste, but also to imagine the nation in relation to the individual experience of a new global modernity. A global modernity intimately connected to the Cold War.

The fourth chapter begins by noting that the reintegration of national symbols went beyond the political and diplomatic concerns of the hosting of the Olympics. The Japanese flag and the 'national anthem' (Kimigayo) became increasingly visible in the lives of young Japanese, but not in direct connection to the state. Individual freedom and democratic expression were now connected by the media to the spaces and places of entertainment and consumption and it was here that these divisive national symbols were reintegrated into national subjectivity. The idea of a national identity separated from the experience of everyday life gradually became more difficult to sustain as the Vietnam War increased in intensity. Student protesters sought to reconcile the external elements of national subjectivity with the internal dilemmas thrown up by rapid social and economic change.[40] By the late 1960s, the contradictions inherent in the country's postwar economic growth were driving much of the discourse in the popular media. Student and anti-war protests were inseparable from the international context of the late 1960s, but intimately tied to the individual experience of everyday life. At the same time, the issue of Japan's relations with the rest of Asia and the domestic and international problems epitomized by the status of Okinawa created a discourse that wedded that experience with the complex and ambiguous relationship between the national and the international in the context of the promotion of consumer society.

I conclude by discussing the nature of the cultural nationalism that emerged through the so-called theories of Japaneseness (*nihonjinron*) in the 1970s and became a consumer-driven phenomenon in the 1980s. To understand the popular appeal of this form of particularistic, cultural nationalism it is essential to understand the transformative influence of the growth of the popular media and consumer society on the imagining of national identity and nationalism. The relentless consumerization of individual subjectivity was matched by that of national identity because developmental nationalism connected the economic transformation of the country to the everyday lives of the people. I argue that, to better understand this process, it is essential to go beyond the usual binary notions of civic versus ethnic nationalism. We need to consider the important ways in which the debate, discussion and presentation of the 'consumer as king' in popular magazines formed a matrix within which individual subjectivity and national identity came together to press what I call national subjectivity. The individual was free to choose the meaning and importance of national symbols and the strength and nature of the imagined community of postwar Japan.

1

Consumer Society and the Media

Consuming the Cold War

In the Taisho and early Showa period, the ongoing process of urbanization, the rise in the number of white-collar workers and an increasingly visible middle class combined with technological innovations, which heralded the growth of popular media to put forward images of changing lifestyles. The outline of the beginnings of a mass consumer culture in the 1920s provoked intellectual and social angst as much as excitement and desire, as images of a lifestyle centred on consumption pervaded the new forms of media and advertising that emerged. In magazines aimed at the new middle classes, the possibilities for the rationalization of the home offered to the housewife and her salaryman husband were opposed to the activities and desires of the modern boys and modern girls who were the dangerous youthful incarnation of this consumerism. The promotion of middle-class lifestyles, the connection of consumerism to everyday life and its portrayal as an essential element of the economic development of Japan have transwar origins.[1]

In the 1920s, the process of rationalization in industrial production brought calls for the modernization of material life and one of the most significant movements of the 1910s and 1920s was the pursuit of a better standard of living through the promotion of the increasing use of household appliances (*Seikatsu Kaizen Undō*). As the 1920s gave way to the increasingly belligerent 1930s, the acquisition of these electrical appliances became a means for achieving rationalization in household activities in the service of the nation. In this context, the Life Improvement Union stressed that 'removing all waste from the home, taking away all ornaments, introducing more rationalisation, we must promote efficiency in the activity of the nation, and contribute to the growth of the national fortune'.[2] Louise Young notes how in the 1920s the department store presented the modern in Japan as reflected in the collection of consumer goods on offer inside. This substituted the daily practices of private life for earlier definitions of modernity associated with the public institutions of the nation state such as railways, parliamentary democracy or a colonial empire.[3] Now, with the increase in white-collar jobs, the expansion of the rail network due to urbanization and the development of the department stores that were often attached to local railway stations, the basis for a mass consumer society began to take shape. Yet it was only as a result of the period of high-speed economic growth, from the late 1950s and through the 1960s, that the possibility to participate in a society based on the consumption of consumer goods was open to the majority of Japanese.

The consistent image of electric appliances in the home, evident by the late 1950s, and epitomized by the electric rice cooker, did not appear before the war. Moreover, the increasingly effective promotion of domestic electric appliances that appeared from the mid-1950s was not positioned as an extension of the life-improvement movement of the prewar period.[4] Nevertheless, in the late 1940s and early 1950s, the dominance of the black market in everyday life served to politicize domestic consumption. Consumption was about balancing the identities of consumer, producer, citizen (*shimin*), and national (*kokumin*).[5] The acts of buying and consuming goods were inseparable from the blunt necessities of staying alive. In this context, during and after the Occupation, housewives' groups turned into effective political actors through their protests for improved food rationing and by rallying against the ever-increasing prices of daily necessities.[6] Into the early 1950s, consumption continued to be an essential aspect of family life. Gradually, through advertising and the popular media, it became a necessary part of the social role of the Japanese housewife.[7]

In the 1950s and 1960s, popular magazines emerged selling lifestyles that opened up new possibilities to a new generation of Japanese and which had, due to the war, been off limits for political and economic reasons to their parents and grandparents. By the late 1950s, the consumer was already emerging in the popular media as the dominant aspirational identity for housewives, salarymen and young single Japanese with disposable income. By 1960, increasing affluence and a burgeoning popular media began to merge consumerism with ideas of nation, and these ideas were compounded by the impact of the Cold War in Japan. In the 1950s, the debate over consumption in the mass media gradually came to reflect the issues of peace and democracy and Japan's importance in the promotion of Cold War–free world values. This made clear a shift in the boundaries of, and between, consumerism, ideas of nation and individual subjectivity. This chapter will provide a brief overview of the political and economic concerns behind this cultural shift and outline the emergence of a media which responded to and promoted, but was nevertheless dependent on, this consumerism.

Distributing the fruits of productivity

The Korean War provided a critical boost to the Japanese economy and helped to cement Japan's position as the pivot of America's defence strategy in Asia. The textile, construction, chemical, metal, communications and automotive industries benefited enormously from war procurements. As Michael Schaller puts it, Japan became 'one huge supply depot' serving US aims on the Korean peninsula.[8] The war took on the role of 'Japan's Marshall Plan' and at the same time established the boundaries of containment in Northeast Asia.[9] In the opinion of the Japanese prime minister of the time, Yoshida Shigeru, the war completely transformed the Occupation's approach to Japan and the situation in the Far East, and spurred the growth of Japanese production over the next decade.[10] Nevertheless, Japanese politicians and economists, along with US Cold War strategists, needed to find ways of perpetuating economic growth after the wartime boom. The war had required the increased production of raw materials, equipment and consumer goods to keep pace with the country's expanding industry and consumption demands, but the focus on heavy industry proved problematic by the mid-1950s when the surge in demand dropped off. Eventually, 'a program was needed which would systematically attack the basic problem of low productivity and high costs throughout Japanese industry'.[11] With less need for armaments and heavy industrial goods, new methods of production, along with ways and means of stimulating domestic demand, became necessary.

These were identified and developed under the guidance of the Japan Productivity Centre (nihon seisan-sei honbu), or JPC, established with

American assistance in 1955. The first such 'productivity group' had been set up in Britain in 1948 with the assistance of Marshall Aid.[12] The economic theory behind the JPC was closely tied to American Cold War ideology. Its original aim was to increase labour and management productivity, a goal that would bring about the expansion of markets, help to increase employment and raise wages as well as standards of living.[13] The ideas behind the programme began to circulate in Japan towards the end of the Occupation in the late 1940s. Taylorist ideas of rationalization, developed and expanded in the 1920s and 1930s, were put to work to enhance productive efficiency and transcend class conflicts that could arise from scarcity. In the impoverished conditions of early Cold War Europe, the United States promoted the purportedly apolitical solution of productivity to combat communism by shifting the focus of the dialectic from class-versus-class to one of waste and abundance. The productivity movement eventually came to be seen as a way of defeating communism while promoting the American way of life. The Ministry of Trade and Industry had proposed a Japan Productivity Centre as early as 1951, but it was in 1953 that US officials offered to promote the programme in Japan. In the same year, the Dōyūkai director Gōshi Kōhei, later to become the third chairman of the JPC, visited Europe and confessed to being very impressed by the ideological success of the programme.[14]

Increased efficiency in the production of goods and services as well as improved technology and methods of organization and operation would strengthen the Japanese economy and raise the living standards of the Japanese people.[15] Promoting the belief that the goal of rapid growth in gross national product was tied to improvements in productivity, the United States had, by the time of the JPC's inauguration, already welcomed tours by some 16,000 European managers, technicians and labour leaders paid for by the Foreign Operations Administration. US aid had also financed a large series of reports on American productivity in Japan and Europe, and the efforts came to incorporate CIA personnel in the US embassy in Tokyo as well as front organizations such as the Asia Foundation.[16] The three guiding principles of the JPC were: expansion of employment, cooperation between labour and management, and fair distribution of the fruits of productivity. The 'fruits of productivity should be distributed fairly among labour, management, and consumers in line with the state of national economy'.[17] By the late 1950s, the consumer needed to be seen to be receiving those fruits, while simultaneously becoming vital, as a worker, to the continuation of growth in productivity. This dual role was perpetuated through the celebration of consumption in the popular media.

Between 1956 and 1966, the JPC sent more than 600 inspection groups to the United States, in which more than 6,000 people took part. The groups were made up of small business representatives, academics, labour leaders, technical specialists and business leaders who studied various aspects of American manufacturing methods. While these groups did study and import industrial technical skills and know-how to Japan, in the late 1950s marketing techniques were by far the most important productivity tool the technical group personnel brought back. Japanese managers came to see marketing as an essential technology, one that offered, as Simon Partner has pointed out, 'a solution to a problem that had plagued Japan throughout its modern history: how to find domestic outlets for the nation's growing industrial capacity'.[18] Throughout the late 1950s and early 1960s, the strength and wealth of the mass market came to be seen as best fuelled by the spending power of the consumer. This consumption would create a virtuous circle spurring production, which would in turn fuel people's desire to consume more. As the agro-economist Tobata Seiichi put it, 'the masses are appearing on the economic stage, they are the agents of effective demand'.[19]

In this context, the 'bright life' emerged in the 1950s as an ideological symbol, which sought to imply 'the housewife-centred family and the dominance of the middle class'.[20] By the end of the decade, companies such as Matsushita were promoting their electronic appliances as the 'housewives' partner' and linking the arrival of these goods in the home to democratization – in some instances even going so far as to link the promotion of these goods to article 25 of the Japanese constitution: 'The people of Japan have the right to enjoy a healthy and cultural life'.[21] This clearly reflected the deliberate shift in the wider economic discourse from a production-led economy to the promotion of consumption as the ultimate driving force of economic growth. Yet an examination of the popular magazines of the late 1950s and early 1960s shows that it was not only the Japanese housewife or her husband who was the target of this ideology. Magazines pressed the benefits of consumption onto young, single people and promoted leisure activities that relied on the promotion of the belief in abundance and consumption as waste.

The expansion of the mass media throughout the 1950s played a central role in linking these ideas with Japanese social attitudes.[22] As Hasegawa Kenji has pointed out, the late 1950s was a time when 'the spread of popular weekly magazines and compact paperback books, the launching of electric household appliances, and the feverish spread of hula-hoops and Dakkochan dolls signalled the arrival of a "consumption revolution"'.[23] The consumer revolution had helped to produce two images of the United States: one was the powerful, patriarchal America of the Occupation, the military bases and the protests against them, and the other America was a lifestyle choice for housewives or a fashion choice for young Japanese.[24] This was partly due to the decreasing American presence in the everyday life of the Japanese people. After the Occupation ended, the number of US military personnel in the country fell from 2,60,000 in 1952 to 46,000 by 1960.[25] At the same time, the electrification of the home and the advertising strategies of companies seeking to improve the housewives' lot reinforced the America of consumption.[26] Throughout the 1950s, the new housing projects (*danchi*) became symbolic of the democratized family, in particular through the promotion of privacy in the provision of separate sleeping spaces. This connected seamlessly with the liberation of women from housework through the electrification of the kitchen.[27]

Yet the debate and discussion in the popular media, particularly in magazines aimed at young people, went further than merely assisting the Japanese housewife and softening the image of the United States. For the Japanese people, consumption was now presented as an individual choice rather than the necessity of the 1940s and early 1950s. Moreover, the early 1950s ideas of nation based around the tropes of peace and democracy were juxtaposed by the Security Treaty crisis with ideas that emphasized Japan as a growing economic power with unique cultural traits. The rapid growth of popular magazines worked to accelerate the process of creating a Japanese consumerism that tied national identity to the individual through the portrayal and promotion of consumer society.

The media

In Japan in the postwar period, the promotion of consumer lifestyles as a means of perpetuating economic growth and prosperity was intimately tied to the ideological divisions of the Cold War. Yet it also reflected the return of processes and networks established in the 1920s and under the conditions of wartime. In Taisho and early Showa Japan, as in the United States at the start of the twentieth century, the rise of corporate capitalism drove changes in social, economic and cultural life. The emergence of large-scale corporate enterprises brought about a shift from an emphasis on the increase of production to the encouragement of consumption. The movement of people into large cities helped to encourage identification with national culture rather than local customs and traditions. Better distribution and marketing networks, as well as networks to promote consumption, accompanied the rise of mass culture.[28] In Japan, the rise of urban consumption and the idea of a 'cultural lifestyle' in the Taisho period had turned publishing, along with tourism and the movies, into industries in themselves. As the number of white-collar workers increased and their incomes stabilized they became the pillars of support for this mass consumer culture.

Mass general interest magazines, such as the monthly *Bungei Shunjū*, became increasingly popular, but the creation of *King* in 1925 saw the first magazine to reach the sales high of 1 million copies. *King* presented itself as a magazine to unite the people and, according to Sato Takumi, helped to overcome class, generation and gender to unite the nation during the prewar and wartime eras. Nevertheless, by the mid-1950s, when the magazine ceased publication, it was evidence of the increasing segmentation of popular culture as much as the negative aspects of its image as a vehicle of wartime propaganda. Sato puts this down to the advent of television as a beacon for national culture, claiming that 'the "national culture" nurtured by *King* was restructured by the cathode ray tube'.[29] Yet, having worked for thirty-three years to 'hold back the tendency towards segmentation', *King*'s decline was also a sign that the popular consumer culture of the postwar period encompassed a much larger proportion of the Japanese people than previously.

In the period following the First World War, transformations in technology helped to build an infrastructure that formed the basis of much of the media that flourished during the period covered by this book. Magazine and newspaper readership increased, interest in the cinema was coupled with the arrival in the home of radio, recorded sound and the camera. In order for the media to become established as a business it needs the establishment of an infrastructure, printing presses and the ability to deliver magazines to readers. As a consumer product it is important to have a market, and when society is in a process of rapid change, there is a lot of room for new companies to join in the media market.[30] The rapid increase in the media in the 1920s was influenced by urbanization, an increase in white-collar workers and the development of new technology. In the Taisho period, more people read magazines but it was still predominantly the white-collar, urban middle classes that could participate in the growth of consumer society. The rapid growth in the number of popular magazines published by the late-1950s, many of them weekly, was a sign that it was not just that television had taken over the role of unifying national culture that caused the decline of the *kokumin zasshi* such as *King*. The growth of the popular media, within the context of the promotion of consumer society, allowed for increasing segmentation within popular culture and brought individual subjectivity to the fore in the experience, creation and transformation of postwar national culture.

With the advent of total war and defeat in 1945, much of the infrastructure and impetus behind the media and consumer society of the Taisho and early Showa periods disappeared. Following the surrender in 1945, Supreme Command for Allied Powers (SCAP) continued the rationing of paper and printing materials begun in the late 1930s by the Japanese government. And, although well-stocked and well-established American magazines such as *Readers Digest* arrived to instil the discourse of peace and democracy central to the aims of the US-led Occupation, *Chûô Kôron*, Japan's most prestigious monthly journal, managed to re-establish printing and release its first postwar issue in December 1945. The journal limited its readers to 100 pages rather than the 300 seen before the war. SCAP not only rationed access to paper and ink, but as part of its policy to reform and re-educate Japan as an American ally in Asia, it also censored the Japanese media. The leaders of the Occupation deemed it of paramount importance to import and disseminate news of an American slant to the recently conquered Japanese. From September 1945 until the autumn of 1949, SCAP permitted domestic Japanese magazines to rebuild, while at the same time recognizing the necessity of opening up Japan to foreign news sources. Perhaps naively, the Americans in charge believed their own wartime propaganda and assumed that once the Japanese had access to the 'true' news, they would warmly embrace these new democratic freedoms and discard their old military ways.[31]

The leadership of the Occupation carried a belief in the superiority of American culture as a model for postwar Japanese democracy and journalism. The promotion of consumption to help boost the economy and provide for the well-being of the whole nation was clearly evident in US magazines such as *Life*. In 1947, an article entitled 'The Price Problem' argued that 'the individual family's efforts to rise in the class ranks through consumption helped boost the economy and provide for the well-being of the nation as a whole', while other articles equated homeownership with democracy, security and civic virtue.[32] This vision of material life was actively promoted abroad. As Lizabeth Cohen has noted, during the Cold War the idea that American consumer goods would be able to 'win the hearts and minds of the people in the so-called developing world' was combined with the understanding that the expansion of US consumables into those markets would also help American manufacturers economically.[33]

Through the Marshall Plan, the importance of household consumption in securing peace and democracy was promoted in Europe. In 1952, for example, the Mutual Security Agency deliberately shifted the focus of the annual German Industrial Exhibition from heavy industry and consumer goods to focus the US display 'exclusively on private consumption'. As the State Department saw it, the display's content was to be developed 'in terms of arguments for a high-production, high-wage, low-unit cost, low profit-margin, high consumption system' with emphasis on the 'fortunate outcome of American economic philosophy when combined with European skills and resources'.[34] Observers of Japanese economic growth in the 1950s drew on 'the precocious appreciation of prewar commentators', seeing consumer demand as one engine of a national economy 'connecting manufacturers, lenders and consumers in a virtuous cycle of growth'.[35] This thinking was clearly driving the policies of the JPC, but at the same time, in the late 1950s, this cycle of growth became a national goal and the popular media made explicit its connection to America and the prosperity of the Free (capitalist) World.

In this context, prewar Japanese monthly magazines gradually re-emerged not only as part of the community of remorse looking to promote the need for peace and democracy to their readership. At the same time as assuaging feelings of guilt over their own lack of opposition to the events of the 1930s and 1940s, the 'old liberals' behind the creation of *Sekai*, first published in 1947, saw the popular print media as a means to create an 'enlightenment spirit' in the Japanese people and counter the threat that could be posed by any return to militarism by the Japanese state. The Science of Thought group, their activities and their journal *Shisō no Kagaku* reflected the goal of many publishers in the immediate postwar period to connect directly with the lived experience of the people as means of overcoming class divisions and the domination of an intellectual elite. Yet these magazines also helped to feed the appetite for news, intellectual debate and entertainment in a country attempting to recover from the ravages of war.[36] Nevertheless, in the period 1945–1952, the widely proclaimed values of free speech and freedom to publish took a back seat to the very real geopolitical concerns of the late 1940s.

As the Cold War came to dominate international politics and altered the nature of the Occupation, the situation served to constrain the development of a more vibrant magazine culture. Yet, following the end of the Occupation in 1952, newspaper companies began to change the nature of magazine publishing. With the resource base and the infrastructure of popular newspapers behind them, weekly magazines like *Shūkan Yomiuri* and *Shūkan Sankei* began to take their place alongside the established Taishō era news magazines such as *Shūkan Asahi* and *Sunday Mainichi*. Making full use of the rapid editing speed and advertising techniques of their newspaper industry backers, these journals helped the weekly format, already predicted in the Taishō period, to truly emerge as a new type of media.[37] In the early 1950s, by including serialized novels, these magazines began, at least in part, to offer entertainment alongside news and opinion. This move would open the way for the growth in popular entertainment magazines.[38]

Still, it was the transformation in the nature of advertising that really allowed the weekly magazine market to expand rapidly, especially once economic growth began to take off in the mid-1950s. As early as August 1952, the Japanese Magazine Advertising Association had trumpeted the benefits of choosing to advertise in magazines over newspapers because the ads could be more easily tailored to a specific audience. Adverts in magazines could monopolize space, and improvements in technology and the quality of paper gradually made ads in magazines much more pleasing on the eye. Weekly magazines, moreover, offered constant repetition and the chance to associate with the latest developments in technology, international and domestic news stories and even the vagaries of the world of entertainment. By 1956, the revenue generated by publishing companies from advertising in magazines exceeded the money spent on advertising in all other mediums.[39]

The rapid increase in the possibilities for advertising revenue allowed magazine publishing to take off by giving publishing companies the impetus to enter the market and challenge the dominance of magazines backed by the large newspapers. In 1956, *Shūkan Shinchō* became the first weekly magazine to enter the market backed by a publishing company rather than a newspaper group. Struggling to match the ability of newspaper-backed magazines to gather the latest news, *Shūkan Shinchō* managed to be successful by publishing serialized novels and through the column 'Town', modelled on the *New Yorker*'s 'The Talk of The Town', which carried up-to-date, light news stories and the latest gossip.[40] The success of *Shūkan Shinchō* was rapidly followed by the publication of weekly magazines such as *Shūkan Josei, Shūkan Taishū, Josei Jishin* and *Shūkan Heibon*. By 1960, thanks to growing economic prosperity, the coming together of the techniques of mass production, mass advertising and mass sales that allowed the cycle of mass consumption to really take off, the dominance of the newspaper-backed weekly magazine was broken.[41]

According to *Shuppan Nenkan* between 1954 and 1971 the total number of published magazines doubled and the number of weekly magazines almost tripled. In 1958, weekly magazines made up over 40 per cent of all magazine production in Japan and, by 1960, accounted for 55 per cent. The appeal of these weekly magazines to both the consuming public and the advertisers, then, certainly lay in their ability to quickly respond to 'fast changing contemporary society'.[42] It also lay in their role in shaping that society as they both fed off and fuelled the ideology of mass consumption. The story of the magazines published by Heibonsha in the 1950s and 1960s – *Heibon, Shūkan Heibon* and *Heibon Punch* – neatly encapsulates the connection between the transformation of the publishing industry and the wider political, economic and social changes brought about by high-speed economic growth. By seeking to move beyond the binaries of reader/publisher, intellectuals/masses and even stars/fans, the publishing philosophy of the company behind the magazine brought the rebuilding of the country through the promotion of consumer society together with the emphasis on individual subjectivity and everyday life.

Heibon was the most read popular entertainment magazine in the 1950s and published for three decades until its closure in 1985. First appearing in 1945 as a literary arts and entertainment magazine, it underwent a renewal in 1948 to focus on music and film. Throughout the 1950s, until television became a reality for most Japanese, *Heibon* was the most circulated entertainment magazine in Japan. During the 1950s, it was the most widely read entertainment magazine among young people.[43] From 1948 onwards, its publishers decided to focus the magazine on movies and music because, as the founder of the magazine put it, 'that's it, there is nothing more entertaining for the masses!'[44] The layout of the magazine was changed from A5 to B5 to allow the printing of larger pictures of popular actresses. Sakamoto Hiroshi estimates that, throughout the 1950s, 70 per cent of both genders aged from the late teens to the twenties read *Heibon*. Its readership was spread evenly across large cities and the rural areas, and 'the magazine was read nationwide by both male and female workers'.[45] *Shūkan Heibon* was published from 1958 onwards and *Heibon Punch* from the spring of 1964. The shifting appeal of the magazine reflected the domestic changes taking place in Japan.

Shūkan Heibon began publication in 1958 and, at first, was aimed at male and female readers. Alongside interviews with celebrities and other icons of popular culture, the magazine dealt with political issues and carried articles discussing the international problems caused by the Cold War. Most issues carried a round-table discussion featuring two readers and an academic or journalist, who discussed important political and social issues. There were also short explanations about particular topics related to contemporary events. Aimed at male high school and university students, *Heibon Punch* began in May 1964, seeking to bring articles filled with 'speed, thrills and sex' to these young men, and at the same time take the 'dull daily lives and culture of male high school and university students and inspire them with a new, money-driven lifestyle'.[46] The magazine was more satirical than *Shūkan Heibon* in the way it approached serious topics.

The publishing philosophy behind *Heibon* and its sister magazines encouraged the participation of readers in the planning of the magazine and provided the reader with a direct connection in their daily lives to the films, music and stars that featured in it. For the magazine's founder Iwahori Kinosuke, bringing people together in this way could work to overcome the dualisms (and oppositions) of the elite versus the masses and work towards the promotion of an everyday democracy through popular culture. In the same way as the intellectual members of Science of Thought searched for means to connect with the democracy of everyday life, Iwahori hoped to find a medium that could communicate with readers directly. Similar to the way the housewives' magazines hoped to reflect the views of their readers in their articles and the layout of the magazine, *Heibon* would not simply reflect readers' ideas and desires, but be informed and changed by them. The establishment of the readers' association, Heibon no Tomo Kai, was one means of overcoming the binary of reader/publisher.[47]

The 1950s is often seen as 'a political decade', the 'season of politics' or the 'season of class warfare'– a time when the Cold War opposition between East and West influenced the domestic split opposing left and right in the political, economic and social spheres. As Sakamoto Hiroshi argues, the decade is often understood as a period of transition from politics to economics. The transition is marked by the opposition to the San-Francisco Peace Treaty at the start of the decade and the Miike miners' strike at the end, all brought to a close, and neatly set aside, by the announcement of the income doubling policy by Ikeda Hayato after the ANPO protests had brought down the government of Kishi Nobusuke. Yet, as Sakamoto points out, this simplistic view misses an important element of the social and economic transformation of the country during the period of high-speed economic growth. Many young people did not find their subjectivity as part of the political movements, whether worker or student and, as so often in Japanese history, the 'political' view gives subjectivity to the political, social and intellectual elites. It ignores the rapidly expanding popular culture within which the young people moving into the cities, to find work in the factories and offices of 1950s Japan, also created their individual subjectivity. The youth of what Sakamoto terms *Heibon no Jidai* (the era of Heibon) are better seen as 'one huge spirit of the times' breaking through the binary divisions of the 1950s.[48]

Heibon's readership had a relatively even gender split throughout the 1950s and its magazine empire sought to appeal to a new generation of Japanese.[49] From early 1958, the company began publishing the weekly magazine *Shūkan Heibon*, as the shifting appeal of *Heibon* changed to reflect the recognition of the power of advertising to raise revenue and editor-in-chief Shimizu

Tatsuo's desire to match the speed and presence of the burgeoning medium of television.[50] Yet, in the aftermath of the ANPO protests, the weekly edition began to focus more exclusively on entertainment, and increasingly sought to appeal to young women. Round-table debates concerning political, economic and social issues disappeared from the magazine and popular culture came to prominence. Indeed, by 1965, the magazines' readership was 81.2 per cent female. By 1960, after hosting a male French foreign exchange student around the same age as his daughters and with the arrival from Kansai of his daughter's twenty-four-year-old fiancé, Shimizu started to question his previous ideas about magazine making. Particularly interesting for him were the differences between the sexes. 'Their sense is different, their likes are different, their way of thinking is different and their desires are different. Everything is different'.[51]

In October 1962, he set off on a round-the-world trip in search of inspiration for a new magazine aimed at young men. After visiting the Chicago offices of *Playboy*, he headed to the New York publishing offices of the magazine *Seventeen*. The trip confirmed Shimizu in his belief that the future of Japanese magazine publishing lay in large, visual magazines with entertaining, attractive and informative pages of advertising that would ensure a low shelf price.[52] *Heibon Punch*, the first magazine aimed specifically at young men as consumers, was the result. To create the magazine, Shimizu became a kind of ethnographer of young urban men, regularly quizzing those who hung out on the streets of Ginza near to the publisher's offices. As he explained in 1965, he would walk around watching the young men who loitered in the Ginza, wondering what they read.[53] As outlined above, *Heibon Punch* came into an emerging market of popular magazines that had been steadily built up, thanks to the rapid pace of economic growth since the late 1950s. Indeed, the budget for the magazine was based on its role as a new advertising medium for fashion and make-up companies, car makers and makers of small electrical goods such as hairdryers.

Conclusion

By the mid-1960s, the transformation of the popular media in Japan was underpinned by the Cold War promotion of consumerism as a means of continuing the economic growth spurred by Japan's role in the Korean War at the start of the 1950s. The shift from a political economy geared towards heavy industry and the promotion of production to one based on the promotion of consumer society and an abundance of goods encompassed notions of peace and democracy. Economic planners and theorists looked to redeem some ideas from the past in their quest for postwar economic recovery,[54] but the promise of increased consumption had become deeply embedded in ideas of democracy and individual freedom. As Laura Nietzel has put it, whether in pre- or postwar Japan, 'materiality was always associated with mentality'.[55] By putting the reader at the centre of the publishing process, the magazines produced by *Heibonsha* (later to become Magazine House) connected intellectual concerns over the democratization of everyday life to the rapid growth of a consumer society that began to promote individual choice within the context of national recovery.

The experience of total war and total defeat led intellectuals to question the nature of Japanese nationalism and, in line with the Occupation emphasis on curbing the powers of the state, many began to search for a new form of nationalism centred on 'free' individuals and built on a democratic spirit manifested in the everyday lifestyles and culture of the Japanese people – something the Japanese state had worked to prevent since the Meiji period. By the late 1950s, thanks to the rise of popular magazines, that everyday life became centred on a growing consumerism that connected the individual to the rebuilding of the nation within the context of the global concerns of the Cold War. As the Occupation came to an end in the early 1950s, the process of linking nationalism and national identity to everyday life in the intellectual debates centred on the more pressing issue of food, its nutritional value and the availability and security of the food supply.

2

Everyday Life, Cold War Division and Postwar Nationalisms

From now on there will be huge differences in the historical role nationalism is to perform. At times it will provide great energy for freedom and development, at other times it will be a fortress for reaction and conservatism.[1]

Gushima Kanesaburō

Something old, something new

During the Occupation, the physical and practical task of rebuilding a defeated country was matched by the desire to redefine and rethink the nature and usefulness of important intellectual concepts. This re-articulation of terms such as 'nation', 'state' or 'class' was just as intimately connected to the wider context of postwar reconstruction as the 'democratisation' process set in motion by Supreme Command for Allied Powers (SCAP). Yet the prevailing view of the occupiers, that Japan was a blank slate, not only dismissed the long history of these concepts in Japan, but also helped to mask the ambiguity of the terms themselves. Long after the end of the Occupation, this ambiguity lay at the core of public debate. So much so that, even in the late 1950s, many academics and intellectuals, such as those who made up the Science of Thought group, still struggled to find ways to overcome the elite tone and academic nature of the language they used in their public seminars.[2]

Revulsion at Japan's wartime actions and the jingoistic ideology, which had guided imperial expansion, entailed social engineering by the allies to change Japanese social values.[3] Gradually, the realization of defeat and the growing recognition that the Occupation troops were not as bad as wartime propaganda had alleged helped dissipate the pervading anti-Western, emperor-centred nationalism. Still, at the end of the war it appeared necessary to completely eradicate Japanese nationalism in order for democracy to take root. Immediately after the war, the Japanese had become anti-nationalistic and, in Sakamoto Yoshikazu's opinion, 'democratic anti-nationalists (*minshushugiteki han-nashonarisuto*)'.[4] Even Nosaka Sanzo, an early postwar leader of the Japanese Communist Party, saw the allied victory as having set the course of Japanese history towards possibilities for future democracy. The Occupation had freed the Japanese people 'toward a realization that democracy was in their grasp'.[5]

The purge of wartime leaders and the dismantling of the coercive institutions of the wartime state mandated by the Occupation authorities played an important part in this process. As Mark E. Caprio and Yoneyuki Sugita point out, by erasing 'dehumanizing wartime images and prejudices, the Occupation administration sought to remould Japan and its people in order to create democratic and representative organisations that honoured individual liberties and respect for fundamental human rights'.[6] In SCAP's view, the destruction of the military state was essential. Prime Minister Katayama Tetsu's 1947 call for the creation of 'a democratic nation of peace, a nation of culture',[7] was not only an important goal for the establishment of postwar Japan, it was also a timely reflection of the quest of many intellectuals to overcome the issue of wartime guilt.[8] The whole process of remaking the nation was deeply linked to the questions of the relationship between Japanese nationalism and democracy, responsibility for the war and the future basis of the political system.[9] As Oguma Eiji has shown, much of the language used to discuss ideas of nation in the early period of the Occupation came out of wartime concerns with morality.[10] Indeed, the intellectual formulations and values of many postwar thinkers reflected a 'basic existential engagement' with the modes and structures of thought from the old imperial system.[11] Nevertheless, during the Occupation, the question of how best to reconstruct the principles uniting the Japanese as a nation was juxtaposed with the issue of how to rebuild the country after the devastation of total defeat.

In this context, postwar intellectuals were deeply divided over the nature of the nation and how it should be imagined. The terms of the debate undoubtedly had prewar associations but the changing nature of the international situation also became a focal point for journalists, commentators and intellectuals. Rather than an uncoupling of the key terms 'democracy', 'peace' and 'culture' noted by John Dower, in the years after the Occupation, the discourse over nationalism and the nation incorporated all three.[12] Democracy at home and peace abroad would best be achieved by firmly embedding both ideas within the everyday culture of the Japanese people. This chapter will first outline the intellectual debates over the meaning and nature of nation and nationalism as the Occupation came to an end. The need to check the influence of the state to prevent a return to the authoritarianism of wartime would be most effective at the level of everyday life. The level of everyday life also appeared to the intellectuals to offer protection from the vagaries and rivalries playing out in the international sphere. The second part of the chapter will show how debate and discussion over food, diet and nutrition in magazines aimed at housewives worked to tie the importance of reshaping individual subjectivity and democratic consciousness to the necessities of everyday life and, in doing so, helped to connect individual subjectivity to the wider discussion and debate over nation and national identity.

The divided nation

As the scientist and essayist Nakaya Ukichiro saw it, during the wartime images of the soldiers fighting on the frontline helped bring the Japanese nation (*kokumin*) together, but in the postwar period there was a need for the 'reality of a new myth' that could unite the people as a nation.[13] In this context, the struggle and challenge for many postwar intellectuals lay in the definition of nation and the extent to which it could include 'universal characteristics'. Questions of universality and subjectivity, at the very root of ideas of nation, could no longer appeal to the shared destiny of the empire or the superiority of the people on the Japanese mainland. Throughout 1957, in a section devoted to the liberal arts in the *Asahi* newspaper, the weekly column 'Ambiguous Words' (*aimai kotoba*) took on the task of demystifying the terms of some of those debates by setting out to define the meaning of concepts such as 'feudal', 'progressive', 'modern', 'authority', 'postwar', 'neutrality', 'humanism', 'political power', 'culture', 'freedom' and 'subjectivity'.[14]

The July 5th edition took on 'nationalism' – a term which, according to the *Asahi*, combined 'good things, bad things, old things as well as new things, all mixed up together'. The difficulty of defining the concept made it not just ambiguous but messy, 'with a wide range of meanings'. It could be used to identify numerous ideas as varied as wartime national purity (*Kokusuishugi*) or Asian and African national liberation movements. Ultimately, though, its character depended upon the person defining it.[15] In the media in the 1950s, the debate over nationalism and national identity reflected deeply political, domestic divisions that followed defeat in 1945, and was unavoidably shaped by the ongoing process of establishing a Cold War global order. The messiness was a reflection of the unsettled, ambiguous nature of domestic and international politics.

Any discussion of nationalism must, of course, incorporate an understanding of the world of nations within which any one particular nation exists, as well as a vision of the people's role in the political system. Many commentators did connect postwar nationalism to a peaceful internationalism and the reconstruction of the Japanese economy under the guidance of a democratic state. The nation would be the foundation on which political and social freedoms, as well as individual subjectivity, could be built up. For progressive thinkers such as Maruyama Masao, the reorientation of Japanese nationalism was part of the wider task of democratic revolution and bringing about a new normative consciousness in the Japanese people.[16] Maruyama promoted the ideas of Meiji intellectuals like Fukuzawa Yukichi, who had focused on ridding the Japanese people of their 'feudal consciousness' and implanting a 'European civic culture' on Japanese soil. The Meiji period became significant in debates about the nature of Japanese society and politics, and Fukuzawa came to be seen by many postwar intellectuals as 'the father of Japanese democracy'.[17] But the struggle to deal with the legacy of the domination of society by the wartime state, and the external coercion by different sides in the Cold War, put the concepts of 'nation' and 'nationalism' in the service of differing political considerations.[18]

Despite the merging of socialist parties and the creation of the Liberal Democratic Party (LDP) in late 1955 heralding the apparent dominance of the conservative elite, throughout the 1950s and 1960s, the democracy established by the Occupation forces was in a 'state of flux and openness'.[19] Conflict over the nature of state symbols, such as the flag and the national anthem, served to polarize the issue, but the idea of nationalism as a force for good gradually became rooted in the cultural practices of the Japanese people and was epitomized by the example of colonial liberation movements. Already by the end of Occupation in 1952, what Nagai Yonosuke has called the 'globalisation and militarisation of containment'[20] had converged with strong movements for independence from colonial rule in Asia and Africa to inform the debates of intellectuals, journalists and commentators who sought to tie nationalism to democracy and social revolution and the *Asahi* article waded straight into the debate over nationalism and national identity.

Reflecting deep disagreement over the idea of nation in postwar Japan, the newspaper cited historian Kinoshita Hanji who asserted that the basis of nationalism was the existence of an ethnic group (*minzoku*) living in a shared territory, with a shared culture, religion and language as a basis for political consciousness. According to Kinoshita, this idea of nation emerged in Europe in opposition to the dominance of Napoleonic France and gave agency to the people as the origin of state power. The problem was that, in Japan, a political consciousness rooted in the everyday lives of the Japanese people had been stifled in the latter part of the Meiji period by the increasingly autocratic Japanese state.[21] The Japanese people were left with a strong sense of cultural nationalism, but no corresponding political consciousness and, through the experience of militarism and war, instead of a force for freedom and development, Japanese nationalism became exclusionist and chauvinistic.

The following month, in August 1957, Abe Kozō also used the pages of the *Asahi* to argue that in Europe, as well as in the new nationalist movements in Asia and Africa, a strong link existed between nationalism and social revolution. Such a connection had not been made in Japan because, back in the nineteenth century, the Japanese warrior class, prominent in the Meiji Restoration, had not hitched nationalism to any reform of the feudal system. For Abe, nationalism in Japan had come from the top down and was, from its very beginnings, linked to the desire of the leaders of the early Meiji period for autocratic power. The imposition of nationalism in the Meiji period meant that, unlike in France and Britain, 'nationalism in Japan helped suppress movements for democracy, liberalism and worker's rights'. An active political consciousness had failed to emerge in Japan precisely because of these particular historical conditions.

Writing in *Chūō Kōron* back in 1952, historian Eguchi Bokurō had argued that, following the Meiji Restoration, the idea that the people should free themselves from the problems they faced was very weak. In Japan cultural production was controlled by the upper classes, and the gulf between things that were truly representative of the nation in Japan (*tadashī minzokuteki na mono*) and the ways of politics and culture had widened before the war. The best example of this was the use of the concept of *bushido* as an ideal of honourable death during the war. The insistence on this warrior ethic appeared more as 'a return to feudalism' than a search for tradition.[22] The process of differentiation along cultural lines, which the development of the ethnic nation entailed, had combined with the historical circumstances of Japan's emergence as a modern state and resulted not only in an oppositional relationship with the West that had led to war and defeat, but also to a disconnect between the everyday lives of the people and the nation.

In the *Asahi* in 1957, Abe and Kinoshita both pressed the case for social and political revolution through a 'national awakening', guided by the belief that this would free the ethnic nation (*minzoku*) from the deleterious effects of external manipulation (by the neo-imperialism of the United States or the Soviet Union) and internal coercion (by the state), an argument made by many Marxists at the time.[23] Throughout the 1950s, the 'forces of freedom and development' were represented by the movements for national liberation across Asia and Africa. These movements were held up as models that could prevent a repeat of the corruption of Japanese nationalism. Nevertheless, the 1957 *Asahi* article repeated a point made at the end of the Occupation, that the central problem of how to tie ethnic nationalism to social revolution was connected to the ongoing debate over the 'nationalism of the everyday life of the masses', or what Marxists saw as 'proletarian nationalism'.[24]

All those involved in the debate in the 1950s were concerned with the domestic implications of the stunting of a nationalism informed by a democratic political consciousness in the Meiji period. Not least because, as Sebastian Conrad has noted, after defeat, Japan's history needed to be integrated into universal historical processes that would allow the country's peculiarities to be understood as the result of backwardness rather than 'as the point of departure for visions of an alternative geopolitical hegemony'.[25] During the wartime, ethnic nationalism had been used to justify reaction, intolerance and the oppression of other nations.[26] The discourse in the postwar media traced the supposed deformity in the development of Japanese nationalism back to the Meiji Restoration, and the quest to shape a nationalism that could be a force for freedom became grounded in the notion of the twisted or arrested path of Japanese modernity. By situating the point of nationalism's corruption in the Meiji period, it was possible for intellectuals to dismiss the experience of empire and war, and focus on the defeat as an opportunity to put nationalism back on the right path. Finding a means to overcome this deformity, by building national consciousness on the foundations of a cultural nation firmly implanted in everyday life, would ensure that the Japanese nation could protect itself in the future.

The end of the Occupation in the spring of 1952 sparked furious debate and discussion in the so-called general interest magazines over the role of nationalism in the war, and the best means of ensuring the future development of a 'healthy' nationalism. This was not just an issue for Japan. The domestic corruption of Japanese nationalism and the external conditions driving the rise of Asian and African independence movements were intertwined. In *Chūō Kōron* in 1952, Eguchi Bokurō pointed out that Japan had also played a role in bringing about the historical conditions through which the issue of ethnic national consciousness had taken centre stage in world affairs. The emergence of the national problem in Asia and Africa after 1945 was an expression of what he termed 'the oppositional and subordinate relations within world history'. Japan had achieved its development as a modern country by conquest and 'only through the great sacrifice of many nations'.[27]

In 1952, with almost half of the world's capitalist production under the control of the United States, Eguchi saw it as no surprise that the question of national independence had become pressing in many countries. In the early 1950s, in Eguchi's opinion, the question of 'what comprises the nation (*minzoku wa nanzo ya*)' was in desperate need of an objective definition. The various movements for decolonization were forcing the Japanese 'to become increasingly conscious of nationalistic things (*minzokuteki na mono*)'.[28] To achieve an objective definition it was necessary to understand the concrete historical circumstances which had given rise to the subjective existence of the nation among the Japanese people. For Eguchi the threat of the West in the Meiji period was key. Writing in *Sekai* at the beginning of 1952, Yanaihara Tadao also claimed that, from the middle of the nineteenth century, group consciousness of a shared national destiny brought people together to maintain national independence against foreign invasion.[29] This ethnic consciousness formed the basis for the establishment of a nation state (*minzoku kokka*). For Yanaihara, this meant that, after defeat in 1945, pure ethnic nationalism (*tanjun minzokushugi*) could not totally disappear within Japan.[30]

The danger of this type of nationalism lay not in the threat of domination by the Japanese state but rather in the nature of the international situation. In an article in the *Yomiuri Shimbun* at the start of 1952, Yanaihara warned the young people of Japan that 'the spectre of ethnic nationalism' floating over the mess of Asia 'could bring happiness and prosperity or more misery?'[31] Through its actions as an imperial power in East Asia, Japan had lit the fuse of ethnic nationalism and, according to Yanaihara, the postwar division of the international arena along ideological lines had created two types of ethnic nationalism. The first, 'pure ethnic nationalism', had been brought about by Japan's actions in Asia as an imperial power. Japan had focused attention on opposing the colonialism of the West, but at the same time denied the populations of its empire control over their own state. The second type of ethnic nationalism, what Yanaihara termed 'red ethnic nationalism', was spread by the Soviet Union and had a warlike character, which would pose a real danger should it spread. In Japan after the war, it was this type of ethnic nationalism that had been the first to develop and had driven calls for Japanese national independence.[32] If allowed to spread, the Soviet Union's conception of ethnic nationalism could lead to war, the danger of which 'follows the ethnic nationalist movements of today'.[33]

In an article in *Chūō Kōron* in April 1952, Inoki Masamichi claimed that by the early 1950s the ideological division of the international arena had sparked a reorganization within both nationalism and internationalism. According to Inoki, the usual belief that when ethnic nationalism was quiet, international solidarity could emerge, and when internationalism was weak nationalism would suddenly rise up, no longer held true in Japan. 'In front of our eyes, two types of ethnic nationalism have become indivisible from two types of internationalism'.[34] In Japan an anti-Soviet, anti-communist *nationalism* was combined with an anti-Soviet, anti-communist *internationalism*. This was opposed by an anti-American, anti-imperialist *nationalism*, which was itself combined with anti-American, anti-imperialist *internationalism*. Far from being non-nationalist, Japanese nationalism mirrored the ideological split that was fuelling the Cold War.

The split was dangerous for the internal stability of the country. Inoki believed that in the immediate postwar world nationalism had seemed to offer the prospect of combining with internationalism to form a perfect system. Unfortunately, defeat and Occupation brought a sense of inferiority to the Japanese that had, in his opinion, all but eradicated Japanese nationalism. For Inoki, a utopian sense of internationalism was all that was left of Japanese nationalism. Immediately after the war, thanks to the new constitution, the possibility existed of channelling this utopianism, into an internationalist commitment to peace. However, the international events of the late 1940s had thrust Japan into a greatly altered and strategically important position within international power politics. The outbreak of the Korean War, which at its beginning had seemed merely a local problem, 'turned Japan into a base for the anti-Soviet, anti-communist camp'.[35] Occupation by the United States and involvement on the side of the allies in the Korean War had decided this. It was at this point that the nature of Japanese ethnic nationalism quickly divided into the opposed camps of anti-Soviet, anti-communist nationalism versus anti-American, anti-imperialist nationalism.

After a period of anti-nationalist democratic sentiment following defeat then, Inoki saw three aspects to the nationalistic trend that was developing in Japan. Firstly, the social disorder immediately following defeat was hard for the Japanese people to understand. The second and related aspect was a growing disillusionment with the Occupation. Although greeted at first as liberating angels, there had been a gradual sense of discontent that had begun to manifest itself as anti-American sentiment. Communists, supporters of the emperor system and patriots who saw the collapse of virtue and the destruction of the people's spirit as being due to the Occupation, were all united in the view that it must end. Added to these internal conditions, the anti-Japanese propaganda of Soviet Russia had increased the anti-Soviet mood of the people. But, ultimately, the liberal democratic emancipation promised by the Americans had not been grasped by Japan.

In Inoki's view, if the power of social liberal democracy had caught the nationalistic mood of 'our people's ethnic nationalism', the connection of democracy with social revolution called for by other commentators, nationalism would have escaped from its division into anti-Soviet, anti-communist, or anti-America, anti-imperialist camps. Unfortunately, the Japanese people had become either ultra-conservative or ultra-left wing socialists. Ultra-conservatism pushed in the direction of an anti-Soviet, anti-communist nationalism. The right wing nature of Japanese farmers, who 'with their pedlars, hawkers and hoodlums form the guerrilla army of anti-Soviet, anti-communist nationalism', was a result of the Russian anti-Japanese stance. For Inoki, 'bourgeois window-dressing which sought to escape from Asia by presenting Japan as a Western country', as well as a quiet patriotism which, since the Meiji Restoration, had harboured the conscious fear of Japan becoming a colony of the West, only added to this ultra-conservatism.[36] It was not only the international community that had been divided; Japanese nationalism itself had been split. The split did not just pose the danger of a third world war, but within Japan, in view of the country's recent history, it appeared to present a real danger of internal unrest.

Two major themes emerged in the early 1950s then that helped shape and define the debate over the nature and meaning of Japanese nationalism: First, the need to build national consciousness into the everyday lives of the people in order to create a basis for the political consciousness necessary for a peaceful, democratic society. The need to protect the nation from the malign influence of the state centred on the corruption of democratic development in the Meiji period and would be most effective at the level of everyday life. Second, the belief that the polarization of the debate could be overcome through the connection of nationalism to social revolution and the nurturing of political consciousness. As the Cold War deepened, the level of everyday life appeared to the intellectuals to offer protection from the vagaries and rivalries playing out in the international sphere and from a return to domination by an autocratic, ultra-nationalist state. Problems over the supply of food and the nutritional well-being of the people would prove a useful trope through which to consider these issues in the housewives' magazines of the early 1950s.

Food, power and everyday life

In the newspapers and those magazines aimed at the middle-class housewife, these intellectual calls for a nationalism grounded in everyday life and the development of a democratic political consciousness to ensure the freedom of the Japanese people became linked to the supply and provision of foodstuffs. Reviving long-standing cultural tropes, rice as a staple food was linked by politicians, journalists and commentators to questions of national identity. Through the debate over nutrition and diet, the issue of food became connected to a sense of personal responsibility and freedom of choice that echoed in many ways the call of the intellectuals for the connection of nationalism to social revolution and political consciousness. Yet far from protecting the Japanese people from the rivalries of the Cold War, the debate and discussion shows just how intertwined issues of international politics and domestic everyday life were. Trade with China was boycotted by the United States and its allies, Korea was still at war and Taiwan was in no position to offer food for export. In the 1950s, Japan's food supply was intimately connected to the shifting Cold War concerns of the United States.

By the end of the Occupation in 1952, fear of communism and fear of hunger, poverty and despair in Japan led the chief US negotiator of the San Francisco Peace Treaty, John Foster Dulles, to emphasize the fact that if 'world trade becomes so divided into restraining compartments that raw materials do not flow, that you have widespread unemployment and undernourishment in Japan, the Japanese will go communist'.[37] The United States' food aid to Japan grew and was extended on the basis of Cold War fears. Crawford Sams, chief of the Health and Welfare Section of SCAP, explicitly linked US domestic farm surpluses to the aims of Cold War policy. In his opinion it had become the responsibility of the United States to assume a position of world leadership 'whether we like it or not'. 'So long as our own great country is a farm surplus producing country ... we should consider as long-term foreign aid for peoples of underdeveloped nations that we are trying to keep on our side those programs for our mutual benefit'.[38]

In wartime, the centrality of rice to the diet was a reflection of the power over, and control of, rice-producing areas in East and Southeast Asia. The wartime Japanese state looked to distinguish the home islands from the empire, and nutritionists worked to create a 'national food' that would show Japan as a strong imperial power on the international stage.[39] In Japan after the war, the Occupation forces had managed to erase many of the ideological aspects of wartime life and, although the knowledge and skills of a healthy diet disseminated during the war 'were perpetuated undisturbed',[40] discussion of nutrition and national diet could serve different ends. With defeat and the collapse of the empire, ways of thinking about Japanese national cuisine exposed an altered balance of power. By the early 1950s, they not only reflected the ambiguity of the international situation, but also the need to link national identity to individual political consciousness, and to work this connection into the everyday lives of the people.

Between 1945 and the late 1960s, Washington took on commitments, which aided the establishment of a wide-reaching zone of trade, payments and investments conducive to liberal capitalism.[41] Japan played a crucial role in this system. As the postwar order took shape, efforts to find customers for large surpluses of American grain became entwined with attempts to solve complex political and military problems abroad.[42] The Recommended Dietary Allowance (RDA), developed for the US armed forces and civilians during the war, became an international reference system for dietary standards, and was used for calculating food relief for the overseas population.[43] As D. John Shaw puts it 'food for war and food for peace became the order of the day'.[44] The GARIOA (Government and Relief in Occupied Areas) programme provided $400 million in annual assistance to Japan to buy foodstuffs, clothing, medical supplies, fertilizer and petroleum.[45] Yet, between 1945 and 1952, 60 per cent of economic aid received from GARIOA and EROA (Economic Rehabilitation in Occupied Areas) came in the form of wheat and rice imports.[46] Although this American food aid to Japan helped take care of surplus production in the United States, it actually prevented Japan's participation in the market for Southeast Asian food produce, particularly rice.[47]

By the late 1940s, the importance of Japan for surplus US wheat production was becoming clear. As early as 1947, Oregon wheat producers had lobbied for an independent commission which would allow growers to pool their resources to carry out assessments of the situation in Japan, 'for the purposes of education, promotion and research'.[48] Before the war, global US exports of wheat and flour had amounted to a mere 6 million bushels annually, yet by 1948–1949 the amount stood at 104 million bushels. At the same time, the International Wheat Agreement kept the price of rice higher than that of wheat in the market more generally.[49] Japan gradually became an important importer of grains other than rice. So much so that, by the end of the 1950s, the country accounted for 5 per cent of the world total for grain imports and 8 per cent for wheat.[50]

After 1945, the collection of quotas was the 'area of most direct and intensive occupation participation', and preventing the hoarding of rice and its infiltration onto the black market was a priority for the authorities.[51] By 1950 things had improved, food accounted for around one-third of Japan's imports and the following year this declined to one quarter. In 1952, the government announced a five-year plan to increase the output of domestic rice and other staple foods,[52] and domestic rice production returned to prewar levels. It had failed to keep pace with population growth though. Without the colonies the amount of imported rice was less than half the average of the 1930s.[53] Up to the mid-1930s the percentage of rice in the Japanese diet had been around 70 per cent.[54] But by 1945, the supply of rice had reached near starvation levels at 80 kg per capita per year, and barley and potatoes had become a common, though increasingly rare staple food.[55] As SCAP reported to former US president and chairman of the Famine Emergency Committee, Herbert Hoover, in a summary of the situation in 1946, the magnitude of the food deficit in Japan was 'unprecedented in Japanese history'. SCAP predicted that without food imports the urban population of Japan would be reduced to an average consumption level below 700 calories per day.[56] Things did improve, and from 1948 to just after the end of the Occupation in 1953, the average Japanese consumed just over 1,900 calories per day. But per capita consumption of rice had declined so that, between 1951 and 1955, calories from rice made up around half of the daily diet of the Japanese. In contrast, the amount of wheat in the diet had almost doubled.[57]

By the beginning of 1952, under the banner of free market economics, the Japanese government felt confident enough to remove restrictions on the sale of rice. Prime Minister Yoshida Shigeru claimed the policy of derationing marked the end of the postwar food crisis and connected it to the wider government aim of promoting economic recovery through free competition. In the newspapers and housewife magazines, addressing questions of food and nutrition by invoking the diet of the nation allowed politicians, journalists and commentators to tie concerns over the quality of the national diet and memories of postwar and wartime scarcity to the wider national goal of independence and the economic reconstruction that independence required.

This implicitly harnessed the wartime idea of national diet to the Cold War Free World ideology within which Japan would regain its independence. Yet, in line with intellectual debates over ideas of national culture and political consciousness, the debate pressed individual agency in everyday life as the most important aspect of postwar national subjectivity.

A free people (*dokuritsu kokumin*)

The unstable international situation was an important factor in the food choices of the Japanese people in the early 1950s. A New Year interview with politician Ikeda Hayato, published in the *Asahi Shimbun* in 1952, called for action to provide cheaper rice. At the same time, it proclaimed an end to 'a deep attachment to rice' and promoted the quest to find alternative sources of nutrition for the population. Acknowledging that the end of the Japanese Empire meant that it was no longer possible to import large amounts of rice, the *Asahi* article also recognized that there was 'a limit to self-sufficiency'.[58] Domestic production could never satisfy the dietary demands of the increasing population. On 6 January 1952, an editorial in the *Yomiuri* newspaper noted the fact that the financial conditions of the country and the 'ever shifting international situation' had 'pulled food prices left and right' over the past year. Worse still, the amount of rice the government would be able to import could soon be limited by what the newspaper referred to as 'the crisis in East Asia'.[59] The newspaper raised the spectre of rice decreasing from 55 per cent of the people's diet to 50 per cent over the year, due to what it called 'blunders' by the government.

The August edition of the magazine *Fujin no Tomo* carried a 'Problem of the Month' article entitled 'Has the Food Problem Been Solved?' According to Kawano Shigeto, a Tokyo University professor specializing in agricultural development, there was still a food problem for Japanese housewives but it was no longer about the absolute shortage of food. Kawano explicitly linked Japan's position in the international economy to the place of rice in the diet of the Japanese people. The main complaint of Japanese housewives had changed from one of 'there is an absolute shortage so I cannot buy it' to 'it's available but I cannot buy it because it's too expensive'.[60] It was understandable that the defeat had brought about a decline in consumption, but the poor state of the economy should have decreased the demand for more expensive bread and, because rice was cheaper, the demand for it should have increased. According to Kawano, the decline in the overall level of consumption in Japan and the decreasing availability of rice made it a much more precious commodity.[61]

Now, though, the government's plan to abolish controls over rice meant that the price, given the international situation, would be inherently unstable on the market. Although he did not explicitly mention the dominance of wheat in the food imported from the United States, Kawano did at least note that until 1950, financial support from the United States was overwhelmingly responsible for funding Japan's food imports. He urged readers to bear in mind that if the international situation got any worse, there could be a problem with Japanese exports. This would lead to a decline in the country's ability to pay for its food imports again and, should that happen, there could be a 'return to the hunger and starvation of the immediate postwar period'.[62]

Kawano concluded that the problem ran much deeper than simply the proposed abolition of controls over rice and the increasing price of staple foodstuffs. The food situation appeared stable in 1952 and that was down to Japan's procurement policies. If imports from foreign countries were stopped, there would be enough food stockpiled for a year and then the starvation and hunger of the immediate postwar period would return. For him, that was the 'real power of, and the reality behind', the so-called stability of the food situation in Japan. In such a context, being self-sufficient was the best form of national defence, and Kawano even equated it with the issue of rearmament. The nature of the Japanese diet went way beyond the simple question of 'the control over or the price of rice'.[63] This direct connection of an important and pressing aspect of the everyday lives of the people to the vagaries of the Cold War echoed the perceived split in the nature of nationalism and national identity in the intellectual debates and discussion.

Yet, in the January 1952 edition of the housewives' magazine *Fujin Kōron*, politician Ikeda Hayato attempted to disavow the wider economic and strategic causes of the decline in rice consumption, and urged a rethink over the nature of the 'traditional' Japanese diet. Ikeda was a firm believer in the power of the free market and, through his appearances in the written media, helped to make explicit the connection between Japan as an independent nation of the 'free world' and the subjectivity of individual Japanese as autonomous individuals. He assured his *Fujin Kōron* interviewer, journalist Hiramura Taiko, that government controls over the distribution of rice would definitely be eased over the coming year and explicitly linked the issue to the end of the Occupation. In Ikeda's view, there was a need for an 'autonomous Japanese people' because Japan would need to take responsibility on the world stage as an 'autonomous (free) country' (*dokuritsu koku*). Echoing the debates of the intellectuals in the 'general interest' magazines, Ikeda urged the Japanese people to establish what he termed an 'independent national lifestyle' (*dokuritsu kokumin seikatsu*).

In the interview, he argued that the government was doing its best to ease any shortages of rice by increasing imports to keep the price down. But he acknowledged that the cost and availability of rice, particularly in the cities, continued to be a major problem. The implementation of free market policies was essential to tackling shortages and the best method of overcoming the problems of consumption, distribution and, most importantly, quality. But Hiramura was concerned that the end of government controls over rice would not improve quality or availability. In her view, relaxing economic controls over the market in rice could result in an even more uneven distribution of food. In the immediate aftermath of the defeat, people from urban areas had regularly travelled to the countryside to barter and exchange goods for food and introducing a free market in rice could mean that those in the countryside would be able to get hold of more rice than the people in the cities.

Both Ikeda and Hiramura agreed that this domestic inequality in food distribution was something that needed to be avoided. Ikeda, however, did not see the policy of de-rationing as the problem. He pointed to the quite significant inequalities that already existed under the controlled system. While in Tokyo only fifteen days' worth of rice was given out each month, in more rural Niigata the amount was twenty-five days' worth. On the black market this resulted in a price differential of eighty yen. Somebody was pocketing the profit and Ikeda was adamant that 'in the situation where we are about to become a free people (*dokuritsu kokumin*) I do not want this inequality as a precondition (*zentei toshite*) of our independence'. He emphasized the fact that the 'present law is criminalising most of the Japanese people'. After all, 'is there anyone in the cities who has not sold rice on the black market?'[64]

For Hiramura, that sounded like surrender to disorder – 'because there is some disorder now, let's make everything disordered!' She found it timely to remind the politicians that those at the bottom of society could not even afford to buy their rationed amount of rice. So even though the government had raised the amount of rice it had procured, and according to Ikeda would easily be able to solve any problems of distribution, many people would be unable to afford to eat it anyway. For Hiramura, it was hard to see how the release of controls over rice would help. Nevertheless, Ikeda was convinced that free market economics was the best way forward and that the problem could be solved by better procurement and improved distribution. In his opinion, if the government were able to provide enough imported rice the price would not increase too much. If it did increase, the government would do all it could to make it cheaper.

As Laura Hein has shown, leading economists pushed postwar ideals through individual economic responsibility, seeing 'household economics as one of the important ways in which democracy and peace could be safeguarded'.[65] Ikeda's interview tapped into this elite discourse and helped to blur the boundaries between national and individual subjectivity. The most important thing for Ikeda, and the development of the economy, was the promotion of individual choice. If the price of rice increased and wheat became cheaper, he believed people could 'think and economise for themselves', and decide what was best to eat.[66] The explicit connection of democracy, individual subjectivity and the international situation in these debates tied national identity to the everyday lives of the people through diet and nutrition.

Food was what the people required, and, for the government, promotion of the free market would provide this. The notion of individual responsibility was essential to this task. To strengthen his argument for the workings of the free market, Ikeda attacked those who had criticized the de-rationing of fish and vegetables. He pointed out that the result of the relaxation of controls over those foods had been 'an improvement in their quality and quantity through the free market'. In much the same way, the de-rationing of rice would push farmers to produce better quality, more nutritious rice, and simple market economics would mean that 'if good rice is expensive and bad rice is cheap it is economical behaviour for farmers to produce more good rice'. Hiramura wasn't too convinced though, and the exchange continued:

> **Hiramura:** That maybe the case for the producers but, as for the consumers, given the present impoverished conditions, rich people will be able to afford to eat domestically produced rice, while the poor will have to take foreign imported rice along with wheat, roots and shoots.
>
> **Ikeda:** That is natural. I think that is the basis of economics. If politics ignores that it will not be good politics.
>
> **Hiramura:** If that happens through a natural laissez-faire policy is it not the job of politics to put a stop to it?[67]

Despite his professed belief in the rationality of the people in the face of a free market, Ikeda believed in an irrational cultural attachment to rice that the Japanese people needed to overcome. In response to Hiramura's concerns over domestic equality and the free market, he admitted that for him the biggest challenge was to change the pattern of the Japanese diet. Rice was essential, but Ikeda stressed the importance of side dishes. Using the analogy of rail travel, he admitted that, as Hiramura had argued, if people only ate rice, free market reforms would lead to the rich travelling first class, while the poor would be stuck in third class. It was his intention as a politician to see to it that everybody was able to travel in first class and providing foods other than rice was an important step towards this goal. Moreover, Ikeda explicitly linked a change in the eating habits of the Japanese people to the improvement of the national economy. All the efforts of the government and the people had to be focused on the international stage to increase and develop the country's exports:

> Our priority is to make this country an independent trading nation. To this end, whether we like it or not, I predict we need to change the pattern of our eating lifestyle (*shoku seikatsu*). Through this, Japanese people will be gradually released from a reliance on rice, bringing bread into the diet and, in this way, at the same time as increasing the number of calories consumed, we will improve the physique of the people.[68]

Soba noodles, bread and butter, and the sweet potato offered the means to survive relatively cheaply. Yet the availability and accessibility of food nevertheless became profoundly linked to the economic position of postwar Japan. Ikeda related this directly to the future economic development of an autonomous country. This required an autonomous people. The Japanese needed to become independent, responsible for themselves and their household budgets, just as the country needed to take its place on the international stage. The government felt that food issues could be solved through the introduction of a free market, accompanied by a change in the eating habits of the Japanese people. Yet the need for a change in eating habits was not simply a political response to temporary problems with the availability of rice, or the need to combat black market racketeering. It became closely linked to the idea of a 'free Japan' and linked the wartime discussions of national cuisine directly to the Cold War concerns of the Japanese state. Division in the international arena practically shaped the debate over the nature of nationalism, the nation and political consciousness.

Bitter Rice

In 1952, Japanese cinemagoers flocked to see *Bitter Rice,* a 1949 Italian film starring Silvana Mangano. The film, which was nominated for an Academy Award for best story in 1950, follows workers in the rice fields of the Po Valley in the north of Italy after the war. Two small-time thieves, Francesca and Walter, befriend Silvana, a peasant rice worker. Francesca persuades Silvana to find her work in the rice fields, which, with the help of the other workers, she does. Silvana falls in love with the crook Walter, however, and he persuades her to help him steal rice from the storehouses during the festival following the end of the growing season. After helping Walter, Silvana is overcome with guilt, and a deep sense of her betrayal of the other women workers. A guilt that leads her to take her own life as recompense. The film closes with the women who work in the fields taking the rice they have received and, one by one, covering her body before walking away from the rice fields and returning to their home towns.

The film was a great success in Europe and made a star of the lead actress Silvana Mangano, who brought more than just her acting ability to brighten the lives of audiences of the time. On its release in Japan in 1952, it also caught the popular imagination. According to a review of the film in the *Asahi Shimbun*, the 'overpowering fleshiness' of the actress in the eponymous role of Silvana (Silvana Mangano) could be taken in two ways. While she 'sparkles with feminine beauty' throughout the film, she is also a daydreamer, who nevertheless 'bursting with flesh' 'efficiently goes about the demanding work of the rice fields'.[69] According to the review, the film could also be appreciated in Japan on a deeper level than simply entertainment. The reviews claimed that because it was set in a rice producing area, the film, which in the words of one reviewer 'does not turn away from [addressing] the times', would be easily understood by Japanese people. Critic Hazumi Tsuneo, writing in the magazine *Fujin Gahō*, believed it would appeal to 'anybody who watched it'.[70]

On one level the reviews and the images of the film's leading lady – usually standing knee deep in a rice paddy wearing torn tights, a tight sweater and tighter shorts – spoke to ideas of the ancient centrality of rice in the diet and culture of the Japanese. A clear example of what Emiko Ohnuki-Tierney sees as the commodity of rice itself being a 'dominant metaphor' for the Japanese people and the nation.[71] Certainly for the reviewers, the film reinforced the role of rice as the symbolic link between land, self, community and polity through consumption and ritual. But, in this case, Silvana also symbolized hard work and perseverance in a period of scarcity and insecurity. For audiences in Japan, *Bitter Rice* could be a reflection of deeply held Japanese values, but, at the same time, a representation of the values required to recover from the experience of war and Occupation.

There were many aspects of the film that the reviewers did not dwell on. The dingy and Americanized Walter and Francesca are criminals. The women in the rice fields are overworked and ill-treated but simply happy to have work. A mass brawl breaks out between the legal and illegal women workers, and Silvana's attraction to the violent Walter ends in death for both of them. Given the harsh conditions which remained a reality for many Japanese in early 1952, it is hard to imagine that many cinemagoers saw the film as a positive portrayal of agricultural work, or even an incentive to work hard for the reconstruction of the nation. In the final scene the women workers do not return to their local towns and villages with their hard earned rice. They leave the rice and the rice fields behind them.

The film offers a powerful critique of American culture and capitalist exploitation. But, according to the reviews, Silvana was much more than an efficient worker in the rice fields providing sustenance for the community in times of scarcity. She was also physically attractive, healthy and robust – 'bursting with flesh' or 'fabulously fleshy' as the *Asahi* explained. At a time when the supply of food was only slowly beginning to recover from the deprivations of wartime, Silvana was a model of health and well-being, whose sacrifice allowed the rice workers to finally break the central grip the commodity held over their lives. In Japan, as the Occupation came to an end, the popularity of the film *Bitter Rice* hinted at the broader questioning of the role of rice in the Japanese diet, and the attempts to link social revolution with nationalism, political consciousness and everyday life in the context of the country's place in the Cold War.

The *Asahi Shimbun* review appeared next to an article proclaiming the establishment of the joint US-Japanese Association for the Promotion of Japanese Health. This international group of researchers and specialists in diet and nutrition came together in Tokyo to tackle problems with the nutritional content of the Japanese diet. The association was a cooperative venture between Japan and the United States with a budget of 1 million yen per month, and aimed to find ways of putting into practice ideas to improve the nutritional value of the food available to the Japanese people. Within the first few months of the US-led Occupation, SCAP had ordered research into the nutritional value of the Japanese diet.[72]

The provision of a subsistence food supply adequate enough to keep mass starvation at bay fitted well in the early years of the Occupation with the policy of democratization and demilitarization. There was little desire to help the former enemy, and the Occupation authorities treated food shortages as a matter of low priority. This policy changed drastically by mid-1947, however, and American food imports became the most basic component of US attempts to reindustrialize the Japanese and West German economies.[73] By 1949, spurred by the surprisingly rapid recovery of European agriculture, world food production had at last moved into surplus. As a consequence, the amount of food Japan could import increased and the government began to relax food controls. Potatoes, sweet potatoes and wheat were all de-rationed in September of 1949, and the nutritional value of food rations finally reached the level necessary to sustain a healthy life.[74]

By the end of the Occupation, with the pressing need, in view of the international situation, to imagine a 'Free Japan', the stature and lifestyle of the people became an important focus for housewives' magazines and the major newspapers. Silvana's 'fabulously fleshy' physique was important in the context of increasing comparison with the nutritional value of the diet in other countries and, in the newspapers and housewives' magazines, reinforced government calls for a change in the Japanese diet. With the passing in 1952 of the Law for the Improvement of Nutrition, which led to national surveys to raise awareness of the importance of nutrition and to improve the physique of the Japanese people, nutritional education in postwar Japan became modelled on the Western pattern.[75] Yet the implementation of this push to improve the diet of the Japanese people was by no means solely a top-down transformation.

While the prewar militarization of nutrition saw the nation's diet as one element of state-driven national and military mobilization, in the postwar period the sustenance it provided, as well as the nature of that diet, became tied to a vision of an autonomous country. This brought together national and individual subjectivities because the 'democratisation of everyday life' allowed the popular media to imagine a Japan of free individuals working towards the strengthening of the nation. In the early 1950s, Japan was heavily reliant on food imports, mainly from the United States and, in the popular media, the debate centred national identity on individual choice and responsibility, not in opposition to state-driven nationalist rhetoric, but as one facet of a Cold War transformation of nationalism and national identity more broadly. Politicians, journalists and commentators evinced ideas of a strong and healthy nation through discussion of the health and physique of the Japanese people, but the debate blurred the boundaries of individual and national subjectivity by linking individual choice, at the dinner table and in the kitchen, to 'Japan' as a prosperous 'free world' nation.

There was no longer a threat of mass starvation by 1952, and, as Ikeda insisted in *Fujin Kōron*, the government hoped to push ahead with the de-rationing of rice. But the nutritional content of the food the people consumed remained a focus for the popular media. Hiramura Taiko had pointed out to Ikeda that even if the rationing of rice ended, many people in the cities could still not afford to buy their allocated amount of rice. Nor was it necessarily the case that white rice was the best staple food from a nutritional point of view. Within the discussion and debate over the national diet in 1952 most of the emphasis was on the need to move away from rice as a staple food.

In an article entitled 'The Rationalisation of Eating with Vitamins at the Centre: The New Style of Cooking Dietetics', Inagaki Naganori, a professor of agriculture from Ochanomizu University, reiterated that since the end of the war the Japanese diet had improved in terms of the amount of food consumed, yet the same could not be said for the quality of that diet. People were consuming enough calories for an active lifestyle, but calorific content was not the only important factor for a healthy lifestyle.[76] Inagaki argued that people should not yearn for a prewar diet of white rice and white sugar. Such a desire ignored the fact that during the wartime the government had ordered the mixing of rice, and white rice was not eaten for much of the period. White rice had for a long time been considered a luxury item and, in an era of wartime shortages, eating brown rice was stressed as the antidote to many health problems.[77] Indeed by the end of 1939, the government banned the consumption of polished white rice and the people were urged to use unpolished rice and mix it with other grains.[78] Inagaki also warned of the risk of diseases such as beriberi and pointed out that it was not good to return to such a diet.

Just like Ikeda and other commentators, sociologist Shimazu Chitose, writing in a special section of the July edition of *Fujin Gahō* dedicated to daily lifestyles and particularly diet, the preponderance of rice in the diet was part of the problem. Shimazu pointed out that in 1952 a Japanese adult living in the city consumed only 1,974 calories. Of this, almost 80 per cent of their daily intake of calories came from cereals. According to Shimazu, the 1,359 calories attributed to rice was an unusually high figure, and contributed to a startling lack of protein, calcium, vitamins B1 and B2 as well as vitamin C.[79] Despite the fact that the food supply was relatively stable compared to the early postwar period, many important nutritional aspects were still missing from the Japanese diet. This nutritional paucity was having a direct effect on the people because of a lack of variety.

Shimazu connected the effects of a poor diet on the physique of the Japanese people to wider economic conditions and saw the improvement of the economic position of the country as essential to the improvement of nutrition. The article presented a typical Japanese family and outlined the best means of economizing the household finances in order to maximize the quality of the diet. Rice was the cheapest option in terms of its calorific content, and while bread was becoming more readily available, the cost of butter, margarine and ham made it an expensive choice in the quest for a nutritious meal. The poor physique of the people was, as far as Shimazu was concerned, clearly a result of the low level of earnings of the people. 'With Japanese workers' earnings being one tenth of American workers', their food lifestyle (*shoku seikatsu*) both from the point of view of calories and nutrition, is weak. A weak dinner table makes a weak body.'[80] Problems of diet had a wider connection to national goals. If Japan were to regain international prestige and standing on the world stage, it was important for the population's diet to provide the people with the vigour, stature and cultural vitality that would reflect that. Yet the country's economic problems were at the root of the bad diet.

Writing in the same edition of *Fujin Gahō*, economist Ōkawa Kazushi asserted the effects of the problems of poor nutrition on culture. He argued that a lack of dairy products was bad for the development of an active, intellectual culture and pointed to the figures for milk consumption in one year: in the United States 192 kg, the United Kingdom 142 kg, Italy 35 kg, but, in Japan, 'only a depressing 1.5 kg.'[81] Figures for the amount of meat consumed and the variation in the Japanese diet also clearly showed that the standard of living of the Japanese people was not so rosy. Ōkawa claimed that the amount of meat eaten in one year was 89 kg in the United States, 65 kg in the United Kingdom, 22 kg in Italy and 7 kg in India, and while Japan's 42 kg was not so bad as a percentage of all calories consumed it only made up 23 per cent of the diet. In the United States on the other hand, excluding cereals or potatoes, meat made up 68 per cent of the calories consumed. Recalling a phrase from the old days – 'good manners begin with a full stomach' – he linked modern good manners to levels of culture and the nutritional quality of the diet. Ōkawa believed that without being able to support oneself and raise children, no culture could begin. Survival and therefore nutrition were essential to enjoy life.[82]

Ōkawa's fears echoed those of the joint Japanese-American body set up to investigate such problems. In March 1952, an article in the *Asahi Shimbun* reported on the setting up of the Association for the Promotion of Japanese Health. On 16 March, around sixty people gathered in Tokyo to discuss the nutritional make-up of the Japanese diet. Their aim was to discover 'how to cheaply and efficiently supply many households with nutritious, balanced food products'. Arimoto Kunitarō, an expert in Japanese dietetics who had been appointed director of the Nutrition Division in the Ministry of Health and

Welfare in November 1946,[83] outlined his view of the problems affecting the Japanese diet. He pointed out that although household expenditure on food had increased, the average calorie intake of Japanese was only 1,960 calories per day. The low level of calorific intake when compared to other countries did not look good against the 3,000 calories per day consumed by people in the United Kingdom, Canada, New Zealand and the United States. It was worse still given that people in Italy, the Soviet Union and Pakistan could boast 2,500 calories per day. While the intake of calories had increased year on year, it was the nutritional vacuity of these calories that concerned Arimoto and the newly established association.[84]

The overreliance on rice and the unscientific custom of mixing it with whatever was at hand was the main cause of the nutritional deficiencies according to Arimoto.[85] Professor S. L. Denning from the University of California pointed out that while the European and American diets relied on grains and sweet potato for one-third to one-half of food intake, in Japan the fraction was closer to four-fifths. The health and welfare ministry had already spent time and money on finding new ways of adding nutrients to rice. The Association for the Promotion of Japanese Health followed on from efforts by the Ministry of Health and Welfare, along with researchers into nutrition, who had recently put into action a plan to come up with ways of providing more healthy fare. The association was aware of the link between levels of income and the poor nutritional content of the Japanese diet. Yet, as the *Asahi* article pointed out, although ideas of bringing more fish and meat into the diet had already been put forward it was becoming hard to ignore problems with the low content of fat, calcium and other important vitamins and minerals making up a Japanese diet still mainly based on vegetables. Doubling of the intake of animal protein had been suggested, as had the idea of using fish to increase the intake of animal fat, an issue that had also concerned the Occupation authorities in the late 1940s.[86]

The *Asahi Shimbun* concluded, however, that 'the reliance on rice in Japanese food production and the custom of making do with what is at hand' (leading to the mixing of rice with roots and shoots) was the main reason for the poor state of the nation's diet. The article claimed that four-fifths of food production in Japan was given over to vegetables. This resulted in a bias in the diet of the people, the results of which had become evident in their physique.[87]

According to the article, a new and more nutritious variety of white rice was being developed, which would be low in cost and contain more vitamins than the usual mix of rice, roots and shoots. It could be cooked in the same way as normal rice, and was apparently better tasting and good for digestion. Once brought into production, this rice would enable Japanese households to increase their intake of those vitamins and minerals missing from their everyday diet without unduly increasing expenditure. Fiscal prudence and good nutrition were important for Japan as the end of the Occupation approached. As far as the new rice was concerned, '[f]or a country such as ours which … exists on rice, this [the development of the new rice] is good news'.[88]

The low nutritional content of the Japanese diet and the physique of the people were linked, and for most commentators it was a backward-looking Japanese culture that prevented progress. As it welcomed attempts to develop new varieties of more nutritious rice, the Association for the Promotion of Japanese Health nevertheless criticized the unscientific custom of mixing rice with other foods such as wheat or shoots to give the feeling of a full stomach. This was one of the causes of the bad Japanese diet and if it continued it would soon become a serious problem for 'the health and physique of the people'.[89] The *Asahi* articles, Shimazu's discussion of the poor nutritional value of the Japanese diet, Ōkawa's comparisons and Ikeda's statement about substituting bread for rice as a means of improving the diet of the Japanese people all addressed issues of economic growth. At the same time, they spoke to ideas of nation, culture and what constituted Japanese food.

Yet all the commentators spoke of the necessity of increasing the earnings of the people to allow them to afford bread and other dishes. Ideas for increasing the number of side dishes accompanying rice, thus reducing reliance on it for nutritional requirements, became the focus of many housewife magazines during the early and mid-1950s. Shimazu believed that if bread were cheaper or more accessible, 'it would probably easily replace rice'. She believed that 'Japanese people's deep attachment to rice can be seen as coming simply from the need for calories'. Rice supplied calories more cheaply than bread because the foods needed to make bread taste better – butter, ham or cheese – were still expensive.[90] Likewise Hiramura Taiko, in her interview with Ikeda in *Fujin Kōron*, did not see any deep cultural attachment to rice. Hiramura conceded Ikeda's point about changing Japanese lifestyle patterns, but she insisted that dependence on rice was not a problem of traditional culture. It stemmed from the fact that the Japanese people's living standards were so low.[91]

Conclusion

Emphasis on the daily foodways (*Shoku Seikatsu*) of the people was part of a wider movement, which further stressed the need to integrate Japanese lifestyles into an economic discourse that focused on the need for personal autonomy in the pursuit of economic growth. The 'democratisation of everyday life' helped to blur the boundaries of individual and national subjectivity. A desire to move beyond the militaristic associations of wartime in the presentation of national diet and national lifestyles stressed the freedom of the individual within the framework of Japan as a free nation. Yet this was a reflection of a dominant Free World ideology, which saw national, cultural and individual autonomy within a Free World capitalist block as the best defence against the threat of communism.

There was an overwhelming need to provide cheaper rice and find alternative sources of nutrition for the population. In 1952, the worst of the postwar food crisis was well behind Japan and the diet of the people was considered an important element in the foundations of economic reconstruction. By taking responsibility for their own nutritional needs, the Japanese people could help in the rebuilding of the country. Throughout the late 1940s and early 1950s, the international debate on the role of nutrition and dietetics became increasingly tied to a discourse of modernization and strongly linked economic goals to ideological goals. The overwhelming economic superiority of the United States by the late 1940s meant that those ideological goals reflected the Cold War aim of opening overseas markets to American goods. In this context, the abundance of cheap wheat and wheat flour helped drive the debate over the place of rice in the Japanese diet.

The prevalence of discussion on nutrition in the Japanese newspapers and magazines focused attention on the everyday lives of the Japanese people. What they ate and how they budgeted for family meals was one aspect of the rationalization of everyday life, which linked pre- and postwar ideas of nation. But the discussions also reveal the tension between the economic necessity of moving away from a preponderance of rice in the diet, or at least the ideal of rice as the staple food of the Japanese, to one that incorporated more varied dishes and replaced rice with wheat-based foods. These discussions were a reflection of the economic and political context within which the US-led Occupation was coming to an end and a means of disavowing that context in favour of cultural explanations for Japan's position within it.

The apparently dispassionate, modern, scientific outlook of nutrition and dietetics served to rationalize the economic basis for shifting ideas of nation and national cuisine. 1952 provided an historical moment when the idea of the cultural centrality of rice to the Japanese diet (and thus to ideas of nation) was being challenged discursively, politically and economically. As the Japanese economy improved, the mid-1950s brought the beginning of high-speed economic growth and stable and cheap imports of rice from Thailand and Southeast Asia more generally. With increasing wealth, rice could again return to the Japanese table as the traditional staple food, albeit one which in reality continued to decline in importance. What is important though is that as the economic situation improved, national, individual and gradually cultural autonomy became even more connected to the realm of everyday life and the individual subjectivity of the Japanese people.

3

A Nation of Consumers?

Understood in its totality, the spectacle is both the outcome and the goal of the dominant mode of production … the spectacle epitomizes the prevailing model of social life.

Guy Debord[1]

Peace, prosperity and the 1964 Olympics

On the evening of 19 May 1960, the Diet debated the security treaty between Japan and the United States (ANPO). As the time allotted for the treaty's ratification was almost up, socialist Diet members staged a sit-down protest outside the speaker's office in an attempt to prevent him from reaching the rostrum in the chamber to begin the vote or call for an extension. Seeing no other option, at 11 pm the speaker ordered the police to enter the Diet building and forcibly remove them. The session was then extended beyond midnight and the treaty was ratified without debate, in the early hours of the morning, in the absence of the socialist members of the Diet.[2] Newspaper editorials quickly proclaimed the events a crisis for parliamentary democracy, and, throughout the morning of 20 May 1960, the demonstrations increased as people came on to the streets to protest against the perceived threat to liberal democracy and Japan's independence as a nation state.[3]

Mainstream newspapers were unanimous in their condemnation of the Kishi government. For the *Asahi*, it was 'inexcusably undemocratic'. The *Yomiuri* saw it as a 'tyranny of the majority' and, though most of the press placed at least some of the blame for the events with the Japan Socialist Party, all the major newspapers agreed that the events of the evening of 19 May were 'tantamount to digging a grave of parliamentarianism in Japanese politics'.[4] For most of the rest of May and June, the media supported the actions of the protesters, including the illegal general strike held on 4 June. Yet, on 7 June, US ambassador Douglas MacArthur II held a meeting with the editors of the major newspapers to seek their cooperation in diffusing any anti-Americanism. Kishi did the same on 7, 8 and 9 June.[5]

When on 10 June, President Eisenhower's secretary, James Haggerty, along with Ambassador MacArthur had to be rescued by US military helicopter after around 15,000 demonstrators surrounded their car, Eisenhower's visit to Japan, planned for the middle of June, was called off.[6] Kishi eventually resigned as prime minister and Ikeda Hayato took power promising to separate politics and economics (*Sekei Bunri*). Ikeda proclaimed an income-doubling policy that would promote consumption and rapidly raise the living standards of the Japanese people. From the late 1950s in Europe, the United States and Japan, the happiness of human freedom, through association with consumer goods, was at the core of media discourse on the growth of consumer society. Even in the Soviet Union, under the conditions of 'peaceful competition' that marked a new, somewhat more relaxed phase of the Cold War, 'consumption and living standards more generally came to the forefront of party rhetoric and state policy'.[7] In popular magazines of the time, Free World ideology came to represent a depoliticized America, redefining Franklin Delano Roosevelt's 'Four Freedoms' by, as Greg Castillo puts it, 'transforming freedom from want into freedom *to* want'.[8]

In Japan as elsewhere, consumption became the key to national economic development, improving living standards, and even better labour relations.[9] This chapter will discuss how by 1964, depoliticizing US and Cold War influences on domestic politics, the popular media in Japan served to firmly embed the reconstruction of Japanese national identity within the marketing opportunities presented by a vibrant, youth-led consumer society, middle-class domesticity and popular engagement with the outside world. From the late 1950s, the popular magazines showed their readers what they should be, what they should aspire to, and what they should and could consume. Their sales figures were driven by a growth of nearly 200 per cent in the sectors of the Japanese economy that employed low-waged women workers.[10]

These young, single working women, with money in their pockets and living away from home for the first time, became a new and increasingly prosperous target for the promotion of consumer goods in the media. Along with the young men drafted into factories and sales departments to power the 'Japanese miracle', the aspirations and horizons of these young women were transformed by the growth of the market for mass weekly and monthly magazines outlined in Chapter 1.[11] The medium of weekly magazines was itself based on the ephemeral nature of consumption. Magazines were bought, read, passed around and then discarded. The aspiring middle-class family was presented with the attractions and possibilities offered by a rising standard of living and the need to think through what increased consumption meant for the Japanese people. The nature of the object itself relied on, and promoted, the idea of waste as a virtue and the freedom to waste became essential to the Japanese promotion of consumer society. The young men and women flocking to the cities could, for brief moments when reading these magazines, escape from the overcrowded and still poor living conditions in which they found themselves, even as they became incorporated into the imagining of new forms of national, international, class and individual stratification.[12]

Yet, the chapter also underlines what Miyoshi Masao describes as the 'relentless consumerization of individual subjectivity' in the postwar period by showing how this process helped to merge national and individual subjectivity in the popular media. Through the everyday banality of consuming, the political binaries of the Cold War – left or right, pro- or anti-USSR/US – clearly evident in the intellectual discourse at the end of the Occupation and brought to the fore in the ANPO protests, gradually blurred. As the popular magazines sought to reflect the times, influence society and began to change people's expectations, the promotion of consumer society, at least its free world variant, connected the national and the international through a global modernity that reached its peak in the 1964 Tokyo Olympics.

Looking back on the Olympics in November 1964, the *Asahi Graph* noted, 'Tokyoites saw men and women from all the continents in the world at shopping centres, entertainment places and parks'.[13] It was these spaces of consumption and the prospect for the pursuit of happiness through freedom that the discourse and debate in the media celebrated. Yet, by the time of the Tokyo Olympics, the apparent influx of all things foreign also led to a critique of the enthusiasm with which the country had adopted a consumer culture apparently imported from the United States. This was grounded in fears over the increasing visibility of the young working men, and particularly women, who consumed and populated the new spaces.

The possibilities inherent in the freedom of movement of money, goods and people, the waste of goods and (leisure) time and the rapid pace of social change wrought by an economic policy that stressed mass consumption appeared to some to carry the danger of making 'traditional national culture' obsolete. Criticism of new lifestyles took aim at the aping of American consumerism, just as it did in Europe.[14] In this way, the presentation of national identity in the popular media was part of a global process of postwar reconstruction. Nevertheless, in Japan, the debate connected the negative aspects of this process to the power and influence of the United States, but saw a more secure and mature Europe that could guide the search for a 'Japanese consumer culture'. Individual subjectivity could be found in the freedom to spend both time and money, to consume, travel and imagine the nation in relation to the individual experience of the new global modernity. While the ideological divisions of the Cold War remained, they came to seem increasingly irrelevant.

Ikeda Hayato's government set out to re-establish the centrality of the Diet in politics, improve public welfare and raise the people's standard of living.[15] Ikeda promised tax reductions, and improved welfare and public works projects. The shift in emphasis certainly helped to associate the government with the economic growth Japan had achieved since the mid-1950s and to ease and displace the memory of state force and thwarted hopes for democratic participation.[16] But the popular media promoted consumption and the connection of consumption to questions of culture and individual freedom in these magazines was a result of a process begun in the late 1950s.

The day Japan was coldest

The opportunities for finding individual freedom through the consumption of consumer goods and leisure time in the postwar period was a major element of media coverage of the visit of Soviet leader Nikita Khrushchev to the United States in the autumn of 1959. In October, the magazine *Asahi Graph* carried coverage of the Russian leader's visit under the headline 'One step at a time, one step at a time'. The article presented reports and photographs of the Soviet leader and his wife enjoying dinner with Hollywood stars, visiting farms and markets, and also mentioned that his son and daughter, who were accompanying him on the eight-day visit, had enjoyed a family visit to Disneyland. Khrushchev and the US president Eisenhower had met at Camp David for three days from 25 September 1959, where Eisenhower had stated his intention to reciprocate with a visit to Moscow in the spring of 1960. A photograph of both men shaking hands was underlined with the question, 'is this the end of the Cold War or the beginning of a movement towards the end?'[17]

There were 'hot debates, defiant remarks on peaceful competition, repeated peace talks and relaxed moments as a tourist in Los Angeles, San Francisco, Des Moines and Pittsburgh'. All this during a trip which, as the Graph reported, 'enlivened the news world'.[18] According to the communiqué released following the three-day Camp David summit, both sides had expressed the desire to work together to solve 'all important international problems' and stressed the belief that these solutions should be peaceful ones. From the perspective of the Japanese popular media, the Cold War appeared to be thawing.

There had been much talk of arms reductions during the Camp David summit and these ideas were debated in a round-table discussion article published in *Shūkan Heibon* in March 1960. Fujiwara Hirotatsu, a professor at Meiji University, discussed the history of arms reduction and the latest proposals with two young people, restaurant worker Shinosaki Takako and unemployed Daigenji Shunsuke. Fujiwara explained that the suggestions put forward by the Soviet Union for reducing standing armies, followed by the reduction of arms production and consumption and even the banning, within four years, of the use of scientific rockets and nuclear research for military ends, were wide-ranging but hard for the West to accept. Secrecy was endemic in the Soviet system and it was therefore hard to verify the seriousness of the East's efforts to carry out any reduction. The West, for its part, had come up with suggestions centred on the establishment of an independent international body to verify any reductions on both sides. According to Fujiwara, these suggestions had been dismissed by the Russian media as signs that the West was not itself serious about reducing arms.[19] Unemployed Daigenji Shunsuke saw their point. He expressed concern that the Japanese government was buying jets and strengthening their Self-Defence Forces at a time when the Cold War seemed to be thawing. But ultimately, for Fujiwara, the problem was not the weapons themselves but the level of distrust in the different camps.

The hope was that this distrust could be overcome. According to Nakamura Shōgo, the former head of the *Asahi Shimbun*'s American office, the great success of Khrushchev's visit to the United States 'made one think that the idea of peaceful coexistence had further inspired and penetrated into the minds of the American public'.[20] Ironically though, the Soviet leader and the American president had met to discuss world peace just as the Japanese government was preparing to ratify the renewal of the ANPO treaty. Pressing ahead with the renewal of the security treaty at this point in time appeared to some in Japan to be a submission to the strategic interests of the United States when the ideological divisions of the Cold War were clearly softening. This contradiction was reinforced when the signing ceremony for the renewed ANPO treaty took place in Washington at the start of the following year.

On 7 February, the *Mainichi Graph* carried photos of the signing ceremony along with photographs of Prime Minister Kishi in Washington. The headline proclaimed 'In the middle of the thaw the cold wave', with the subheading 'the day Japan was coldest'.[21] The article carried photos and commentary on the demonstrations against the treaty by university students in Tokyo, and claimed that, since the return of the signatories to Haneda airport there had been no *banzai* or celebration of the treaty. The Japanese government appeared to be going against the grain internationally by renewing a military agreement with the United States just as it appeared to be unnecessary. At the time, when the conditions of the Treaty's renewal became known to the Japanese public this contradiction between the apparent thaw in the Cold War and a wider awareness of the prospect for rapid changes in the security situation in the future only facilitated the growing opposition.

A monthly current affairs column in the housewife magazine *Fujin Kōron* played on this ambiguity and the volatility within the international arena. The article pointed out that the year 1960 had the potential to turn out to be a historic one, but at the same time there was also a good chance that it might not. The article reminded readers that 1960 was only fifteen years after the atomic bombings of Hiroshima and Nagasaki, eight years after the H bomb tests, three years after the appearance of the first inter-continental ballistic missile (ICBM), not to mention two years since the landing of a rocket on the moon.[22] As Fujiwara Hirotatsu pointed out in *Shūkan Heibon*, the Soviet Union had developed an ICBM in 1957, and it was obvious with hindsight that the West had seriously underestimated them. Consequently, even with the apparent thaw and Khrushchev's visit to the United States, 'the military power of the Soviet Union gradually became unusually threatening to the Western side'.[23] According to the *Fujin Kōron* article, by 1960 it was clear that the human race would be wiped out in the event of another war and it was equally clear that, although there existed no other option but to live in peace, 'human feelings do not move in a logical way'.[24] Despite the apparent thaw, fear and distrust remained in the media. The international situation was volatile, but this did not necessarily mean the security treaty was essential for Japan's defence. In many ways, it made the treaty less important.

In January 1960, twenty-two-year-old beautician Tanada Etsuko pointed out that things had changed a lot since the signing of the first ANPO treaty in 1952. These changes brought into question the reliance of Japan on the United States and vice versa. Taking part in a discussion in *Shūkan Heibon* Tanaka noted, 'We can put a rocket on the moon, and we live in an era when we can take pictures of the dark side of the moon. In an era when a missile can fly at the touch of a button the United States cannot guarantee its own security by making Japan a bullet proof vest!' Takagi Takeo of the *Yomiuri Shimbun* agreed, pointing out that if there were to be a war between Taiwan and China and the United States became involved there was a grave danger of Japan coming under retaliatory attack in the form of the bombing of US military bases in Japan. Takagi mentioned the fact that the treaty as it stood had no limits. The next reform would not be due for another ten years, but in such a 'speedy era' ten years was far too long. For Takagi it was 'impossible to think that the international situation would not have changed in ten years'.[25] Japan would do better to keep its options open.

The concept of mutual protection contained in the new treaty influenced the vehemence of opposition to it. It also provided some grounds for the belief that there was a price Japan would pay for its alliance with the United States. Yamashita Hajime, a professor at the University of Tokyo, pointed to the ambiguity in political discussions of the treaty. The thorny but central issue of the definition of the concept 'Far East' was ambiguous. The government's explanation had changed two or three times in the Diet discussions.[26] Yamashita also brought up the idea of prior consultation, the right of Japan to refuse to help the US military as well as the problem of nuclear arms, saying, 'We don't know at the moment if there are nuclear weapons in Japan'.[27] None of the most important issues surrounding the treaty were resolved. At a time of an apparent thaw in the Cold War, the renewal of the treaty was raising more doubts and worries for the people than it was solving. Yet, as *Fujin Kōron* pointed out, one of the few positive features of the renewed treaty was that it expressed a 'new economic cooperation between Japan and the United States'.[28]

Soft money in the Silver 60s

For many historians of postwar Japan, mass consumer society, consumer consciousness and consumer protest developed only after the vehement mass political protest movement against ANPO had brought down the Kishi government. New prime minister Ikeda Hayato sought to double income and promote consumption. To some extent, after years of exhortations to thrift and the avoidance of ostentation, 'the invitation to spend meant an enormous shift in the ethics of consumer behaviour'.[29] Yet, Ikeda's policies were not simply political responses to the protests. The plan was certainly politically successful because it changed the atmosphere from one of opposition to the state to one focused on economic growth.[30] Nevertheless, it is important not to restrict the rapid growth of consumer society and the debate over the nature of consumerism to a sudden and politically motivated, state-driven ideological attempt to make the people forget the mass protests of ANPO. In many ways it was a return to a new normal, culminating in the ultimate national display of conspicuous consumption the hosting of the Olympic Games in Tokyo in October 1964.

Already, in 1956, a government white paper declaring the 'end of the postwar' had celebrated a return to economic stability.[31] Nevertheless, the large influx of workers into the cities during the boom created by the Korean War had made clear the need to improve infrastructure and living standards, in particular by improving housing provision. The state-sponsored housing agency, the Japan

Housing Corporation (JHC), established in 1955 by Prime Minister Hatoyama Ichirō, was given the task of building large-scale apartment complexes (*danchi*) for middle-class urban families. For those lucky enough to be chosen in the ballot to buy one, these newly built apartment complexes symbolized a style of everyday urbanity that became a prototype of middle-class life in postwar Japan.[32] As Ikeda's secretary Ito Masaya noted, the change in focus to economic growth announced was nothing more than the continuation of policies and debates already playing out in the popular media.[33] Consumer protest movements had grown in connection to the food problems of the 1940s and early 1950s.[34] The acceptance of growth as an economic goal and the continual expansion of individual consumption was actually connected to an economic growth that had continued from the late 1940s and appeared to show no signs of stopping. Indeed, the 'income doubling plan' recognized an expectation of growth that much of the public already strongly felt. In effect, it worked because 'labourers, office workers, and not just the financial world, sympathised and were galvanised by the plan for that reason'.[35]

At the beginning of 1959, the *Yomiuri Shimbun* had published a commentary by Hitotsubashi University professor Nakayama Ichirō in which he outlined an economic theory for doubling personal income. At a press meeting in Hiroshima the following month, Ikeda Hayato, at the time out of the cabinet though still a powerful political presence, presented the idea as his 'income-doubling policy'. By the summer of 1959, he had become minister for international trade and industry with the policy firmly at the centre of his political ambitions.[36] The plan was created by the Economic Planning Agency in 1959 under Kishi as prime minister, and work began in the autumn of that year reaching its peak during the security treaty crisis in the spring and summer of 1960. After Kishi's resignation and Ikeda's appointment as prime minister, work on the plan was speeded up with an eye on the general election to be held in November. The text was finally made public in September 1960.

As early as the start of 1960, the *Mainichi Graph* published a photograph showing deliverymen hauling a new piano through the window of an apartment in a new and ultra-modern *danchi* building complex with the tag line 'even the neighbours have bought one'. 'Pianos costing as much as ¥200,000 are being brought to the *danchi* everyday … the symbol of high class for the *danchi-zoku* is no longer the TV … because of the psychological process of the increasing competitiveness of everyday life the *danchi* are the place of powerful mass consumption', announced the caption to the side. The article, published at the start of the era dubbed the 'Silver 60s', reflected a shift to 'powerful mass consumption' as an economic goal and an end in itself.[37]

At the start of the Silver 60s, the essence of a consumer society, according to the popular media, was to be found in the freeing up of the movement of money, goods and people. Doubling income and raising the standard of living were not simply a matter of bending economic policy to political will. There were institutional and cultural considerations to take into account. The *Graph* noted that when an American salaryman wanted to buy a boat his bank lent him the money. In Japan in 1960, people still consumed within their monthly budget and if money was not 'freed-up' people would not be able to spend at will. Waste was key because using things freely meant the creation of waste. Essential to a consumer society, a wasteful lifestyle needed to be embedded within a culture of consumption that encouraged such waste. As the *Graph* put it, 'to develop a prosperity which has no limits there has to be a demand which has no limits'.[38] Yet, for many commentators, persuading Japanese people to 'use things freely' required a cultural transformation.

State officials and others did recognize the benefits to industry in freeing up the supply of money. The availability of consumer credit in Japan had been growing during the late 1950s. Singer, the American sewing machine company, returned to the Japanese market in 1952 and began offering instalment credit from 1954.[39] The availability of consumer credit increased so rapidly in the late 1950s that, in 1959, MITI (Ministry of International Trade and Industry) issued an administrative order restricting the ability of finance companies and department stores to offer consumer credit.[40] Nevertheless, the 'freeing up' of money was proceeding rapidly by the late 1950s. By 1960, monthly salaries were paid by cheque, rent came automatically out of the bank and money was distributed 'without you even having to touch cash'. The *Graph* saw this as a shift from an 'era of hard money to an era of soft money'. It was the key to a consumer lifestyle and would 'continue to make consumption a casual thing'.[41]

It was not just money that needed to circulate freely in order to bring about a consumer revolution. Under the headline 'Lifestyle Progressivism: America – ¥14 trillion on pastimes', the *Mainichi Graph* explained how the technological revolution meant that the nature of work itself was changing. Free time was continually increasing, and, as with purchasing consumer goods, waste was important. American people 'wasted' vast amounts of both money and time. A photo-spread showed people painting by a lake in Aspen, canoeing in Northern Minnesota, a family enjoying time in the garden and a family camping in Kentucky. This promotion in the media of the virtue of free time and free spending, and its connection to individual freedom, was reinforced in the summer of 1960 when the same magazine reported on the boom in boat ownership in Japan. 'Yachting and motor-boating have become popular among the Japanese people recently. Groups of four or five that own a yacht or a motorboat, repair the craft by themselves'. Going out on a boat, 'though it may sound like an exaggeration, allows you to perceive the happiness of human freedom'.[42]

Back in January, the magazine had asked 'What about Japan? … now waste is a virtue, we exclaim with an indifferent smile, if this lifestyle becomes a reality by 1970 it will certainly be the Silver 60s which will have played a role in bringing it about'.[43] Increasing free time, the easy circulation of money, goods and people, backed up by the desire for waste, lay at the core of the consumer society on offer and the achievement of individual freedom. Gradually the attractions of what one magazine termed 'powerful mass consumption' spread beyond the conjugal confines of the housing projects. The act of purchasing goods to fill the Danchi and increasing opportunities for leisure activities and spending for young, single people, helped to create and domesticize an everyday nationalism shaped by the political economy of the country. The media debated the cultural implications of this new lifestyle and, in doing so, worked to normalize the connection between national and international imperatives and the everyday lives of the Japanese people.

The upheaval surrounding the renewal of the Security Treaty highlighted just how powerful the drive to promote the growth of consumer society had become since the mid-1950s. During a round-table debate held in the midst of the unrest and published at the end of June 1960 in *Shūkan Heibon*, department store worker Okawa Michiko succinctly captured the ambiguity of the situation and the importance of overcoming the political left/right binary that has framed much of the historical debate on the 1950s. '(At work) everybody has become interested in the ANPO problem. Before we mostly talked about clothes and make-up now it's all about June 15th and Kishi. Everybody hates

Kishi'.[44] Okawa (20) was joined by singer Teramoto Keichi (27), actress Hara Chisako, 'TV talent' Canadian Lee Smith (18), Chūō University student Fujimoto Kaiya (20) and host Ōya Sōichi.

'When will Kishi quit? Even among people with no interest in politics, in place of "good morning" or "good evening" this (question) has become the extraordinary conversation point', stated the article. The anger and hatred directed towards Kishi was powerful among the young people chosen to take part in the debate. Yet, for the most part, the tone was apologetic when the subject turned to Japan's relationship with the United States. Canadian Lee Smith claimed to be, as 'an individual, a neutral' (her father worked in the Canadian embassy and she therefore 'promised to avoid being political'), but she thought the demonstrations opposing the treaty were strange, in particular the desire to cancel President Eisenhower's visit. She turned the readers' attention to Kishi and the US president. 'I understand that everybody hates Kishi … but why were there placards proclaiming "Don't Come Ike" and "I hate Ike"? I don't think there is any connection between Kishi and Ike'. 'It's not that we hate Ike!' Hara replied and Ōya Sōichi agreed. 'That's right. It's probably hard for foreigners to understand the feelings of the Japanese people right now. I think even MacArthur in the embassy does not understand the feeling at the moment'.[45] Fujimoto stressed that the protests were not 'anti-America or totally against Eisenhower's visit' and Teramoto Keichi hoped Eisenhower would understand that 'the Haggerty incident does not mean we hate Haggerty or America'. Kishi and his anti-democratic actions, not the United States, had been the main target of the protests of June.

Still, the treaty itself also gave rise to ambiguity:

Smith: I understand that Kishi is hated, but why hate ANPO? Doesn't it protect the Japanese people?

Okawa: I think ANPO probably has some good points, but the bad points are worse.

Fujimoto: Until now ANPO has been forced on us by America, but in revising it the Japanese people should be able to give their opinions. That's the problem.

Ōya: But up to now Japan had no freedom to cancel the treaty. In the next ten years, if we want to cut off the treaty we can do. However, if we cancel the treaty unilaterally it will mean cutting off relations with America. That is the problem.

Hara: It's not about saying 'We like America' or 'We like the Soviet Union' I think the hope of the Japanese people lies in their saying 'we want to live in peace'.

Teramoto: At any rate, people are resigned to wanting something to happen soon. Honestly, when I go to the 'Young Japan' meetings and they are all moaning about the anti-America demonstrations … as someone who sings Western music, I feel like giving up! (laughs).[46]

The article allowed readers to sense a gap between the Japanese people and Japanese politics and, at the same time, provided them with a means of considering the events of 1960 from an international perspective. Smith's presence and Ōya Soichi's role as commentator allowed the reader to sense that the anger on the streets of Tokyo was ambiguous. The renewal of the Security Treaty was being imposed on the Japanese people without their consent, yet the protest movement was not necessarily anti-American and the treaty itself was not necessarily a bad thing. The ambiguity created room for the reader to begin to view the relationship with the United States on Japanese terms while recognizing an element of subservience and, as with the wider media debates and discussions, underlining the necessity of the treaty for the economic development of Japan. Smith continually detached Kishi from the Treaty allowing readers to do the same. Importantly, her presence encouraged the reader to see the broader international perspective on the Security Treaty crisis. Japan's relationship with the Free World could have been jeopardized by the protests, but her professed neutrality allowed the reader to sense the benign nature of the international community and merge the United States with the 'West' more broadly. Her foreignness also allowed the reader to consider the unique aspects of Japanese culture that had apparently been evident in the protests.

The feelings of the Japanese people were hard for foreigners to understand so Ōya Sōichi looked to culture for an explanation. He noted that 'the Japanese people have a long tradition of hating Prime Ministers and people in power', and that 'traditionally in Japan, protesters make the police their enemy'.[47] But, the main problem for the participants in the debate, and for the magazine's readers and publisher, was the need to restore order so that the young people could get back to consuming. As Teramoto pointed out, many young people at his performances were feeling unsettled by the seeming anti-Americanism of the protests. By separating Kishi from the treaty, and reinforcing the image of a benign America in the guise of the 'Free World', the debate added to an increasing depoliticization in the portrayal of consumer society. This was important because, as Ōya concluded, 'without peace *Shūkan Heibon* will not sell. For that reason (let's hope) that the end comes and peace returns'.[48]

Making Japanese into world people

The idea of peace and an engagement with a benign outside world was, by the early 1960s, essential to the individual happiness which came from free time, free spending and the free circulation of money. In the popular media the world was opening up for young Japanese, particularly young women. Middle-class and popular magazines presented the lure of glittering global careers, lifestyles and romances. They often featured debate and discussion of the possibilities and attractions of living abroad. Yet, the increasing openness of young Japanese women to travelling, working and living abroad was connected to, even dependent on, the larger discourse of consumerism and individual subjectivity that gained prominence through the popular media in the late 1950s and early 1960s. As Karen Kelsky has shown, the economic power of Japan in the 1980s and 1990s was empowering, allowing 'highly educated middle-class Japanese women … to imagine and pursue, their own self-interest beyond Japan's borders'.[49] Such a discourse could become a reality for larger numbers of women in the 1980s and 1990s, but the internationalization of Japanese women's imagination and self-interest was part and parcel of the process of remaking ideas of nation in the context of the nurturing of a consumer society in the postwar period. In this way, the debate in the popular media offered 'the enticement of modern democratic access to global pleasures such as tourism', and tapped into the images of modern lifestyles epitomized by the air hostess when domestic travel companies expanded their own tour packages during the early 1960s.[50]

At the start of 1960 *Shūkan Heibon* was already touting the prospects for finding the good life in the United States. 'There is a Japan boom all over

America, but all eyes in Hollywood in particular are looking to Japan'. In the United States, a 'weekly wage of ¥36,000 is not a dream'.[51] According to producer Matsuda Kyoko, the next two or three years would offer the perfect chance for any Japanese hoping to make it big in the United States. Matsuda herself was working as a producer at NBC and offered other examples of young Japanese women making it in America. Nobu Azumi, a former fashion model in Japan, had moved to America after marrying an American soldier. Quickly making contacts in America she had become a film star and was rumoured, 'according to newspapers and magazines over there', to be on the verge of becoming the number one Asian star in America. 'If that happened it would be amazing: 4 or 5,000 dollars a week'. To an ordinary Japanese woman this was an unbelievable amount of money, but, as Matsuda saw it, 'there are Japanese women who have those possibilities'.[52] Naoko Shibusawa discusses the way Hollywood sought to use Japanese actresses and actors to soften the American people's attitude towards the former enemy. Under the Eisenhower administration this was closely linked to Cold War concerns for the economic reconstruction of Japan and it also worked the other way, presenting a benign and attractive America to the Japanese people.[53] At the same time, in the popular Japanese media, the need to create a global consciousness came to the fore.

Travelling abroad was presented as an essential component of this. Nevertheless, up to the mid-1960s, it was unusual for Japanese to travel abroad. Passports were valid for only one trip, there was a $500 limit on the amount of money that could be taken out of the country and the Ministry of Finance had to approve the trip. Tourism was not usually considered a valid reason. In any case the cost of travel was prohibitively expensive for most Japanese, so that even when restrictions were lifted in 1964 only 15.1 per cent of overseas travellers were classed as 'tourists'.[54] Despite this, by the mid-1960s, magazines such as *Fujin Kōron, Shūkan Heibon* and *Heibon Punch* were promoting living and working abroad and tourism. So much so that in September 1964, *Fujin Kōron* insisted that it was a reality that there was an increasing 'number of women saying, "whatever the city, whatever the job I want to try working abroad"'.[55]

In January 1964, *Shūkan Heibon* published a travel essay by Kanetaka Kaoru, a Tokyo Broadcasting Services (TBS) TV presenter. 'Kanetaka Kaoru's World Travels' predicted that 1964 would be a boom year for travelling abroad.[56] This was followed in May 1964 by a travel guide for those readers who were 'fed up with living in small Japan'.[57] The world was getting smaller and easier to navigate. *Fujin Kōron*'s readers were urged not to look for cultural differences but rather to 'see the world as one place, like going from Kyushu to Tokyo'. 'From Tokyo to Kyushu takes 20 hours, on a jet you can be in America in the same time. And Europe too'.[58] In May 1964, *Heibon Punch* published a special article on the art of budget travel for young Japanese men. With the liberalization of travel restrictions the 'hearts of young people were bursting' and the article proffered advice on topics ranging from 'women to toilets' by four people who had successfully travelled on a shoestring budget. An accompanying column explained how to save money by staying in Youth Hostels in Europe or the YMCA in the United States. After listing the average prices in the red light districts of several countries – Greece, Turkey and Pakistan – unemployed twenty-five-year-old Tonegawa Masakasu offered his advice to those planning to travel. He urged those who were no good at languages not to travel and those with a lot of money to stay and travel within Japan. Anybody who did plan to travel abroad should 'shed their consciousness of being Japanese' and travel as 'so-called human beings'.[59]

Writing in *Fujin Kōron* in February 1964, Hayashi Shūji hoped to encourage Japanese women to travel more. The Japanese government claimed that their country was on a par with Western Europe, at least economically and Hayashi set out to explore the implications, and veracity, of this claim. Throughout the article, he sought to address the questions 'What is Western Europe?' and 'What kind of thinking governs the daily life of the people of Western Europe?' Travel to Europe was becoming cheaper for Japanese tourists, and Hayashi recounted meeting a Japanese woman in Heidelberg who was travelling around on only three dollars a day. The woman did not speak German, so in Hayashi's opinion the trip must have been difficult, but more freedom to travel would mean more people being able to gain this kind of experience. 'Touching deeply embedded Christian culture and monuments, seeing the remains of the development of civic culture' was all necessary in order 'to make Japanese people into world people'.[60] Despite what the Japanese government said, Hayashi saw Europe as a much cheaper and more rewarding place to live, work and travel.

The reason for this difference in living costs was cultural, according to Hayashi, and it was very evident in the significant differences in the modes and means of consumption that existed between Europe, and the United States and Japan. Japan's main experience of foreign culture had come through the US-led Occupation, and as a result, in Hayashi's opinion, America was the only developed culture the Japanese people knew. In the United States and Japan waste was natural, but in Europe Hayashi believed people were more careful in not throwing things away. The obvious example in Japan was housing. 'In Japan if you live in a house for 50 years it is no longer habitable, but in Europe they last for many years'.[61] Paris was a fantastic example of this, where, according to the author, Montmartre was in the same condition as when it was first built in the nineteenth century. London was much the same, and the London Underground, built almost 100 years before, still served the 1964 rush hour. For Hayashi the lesson was obvious, 'if it is built, build it well and then use it for as long as possible'. Life was 'cheaper' in Europe because people placed more value on what they owned. In contrast, the problem in Japan was the adoption of an American attitude to everyday consumer society. The culture of waste promoted at the start of the 1960s had already come to define Japanese consumer society as far as Hayashi was concerned.

For Japanese people to live at the same level as the people of Western Europe, to 'have central heating, eat luxurious high-calorie food, wear Italian shoes and English clothes', they 'would probably need four or five times the lifestyle costs of today'.[62] Housing costs were more expensive in Japan, but watches, clothes, stationery, leather goods, jewellery and other goods were also more expensive in Japan. In a consumer society this meant that Western Europe was a much cheaper place to live than Japan. For Hayashi, things became more expensive if other people did them for you, and this was a fundamental part of the culture of consumption in Japan. Ignoring the fact that labour costs were much lower in Japan, when travelling in Europe Hayashi's advice to Japanese people was simple: 'drive the car yourself, stay in a *pension*, wash your own clothes and eat in self-service restaurants'. Japanese people thought Europe was expensive because they tried to travel like they did in Japan. The economic philosophy of a developed country (*senshin kuni*) was simple in Hayashi's opinion: 'it becomes more expensive if someone else does it for you'. Japanese consumer society had developed on the basis of cheap labour and that had brought about a culture of service where everyday tasks were paid for.[63] The implication was that Japan, because of its wasteful culture of consumption derived from the US model, was not yet among the ranks of the developed countries (*senshin kuni*).

Another difference between Japan and Europe centred on the concept of a 'European independent spirit'. Hayashi claimed that while people in Europe would deal with problems themselves, the Japanese in comparison lacked initiative and always found it necessary to rely on officials. Japan's approach to solving problems was to create more bureaucrats, and this cost the people in tax. In Western Europe such problems were always sorted out independently. Because Japanese people were 'always meddling in others' affairs', people didn't care about causing other people inconvenience and so they didn't try to solve issues amongst themselves. This led to a situation where the Japanese government treated the people like children, while in Western Europe they were treated like adults. Everyone was free to decide the best way to live but, Hayashi insisted, 'if you don't treat people like adults there will be no independence. In Europe the independence which is at the base of democracy runs deep'.[64] Japan's citizens lacked an independent approach to taking their civic responsibilities seriously, and the high cost of living stemmed not only from the government's economic policies but from a backward culture of waste.

Hayashi's evidence for this came from his experience travelling on a train in Western Europe. As a non-smoker he took a seat in a compartment with six other people. During the journey one man, 'forgetting he was in a non-smoking compartment, lit a cigarette. Very quickly an old woman sitting next to me scolded him'. The smoker apologized for being rude, claiming he had not realized the compartment was non-smoking, and put out the cigarette. According to Hayashi, neither the old woman nor the man looked annoyed and were perfectly relaxed with one another, 'it was a pleasing scene'.[65] In Japan, the economic insecurity and inequalities brought about through the policy of high-speed growth were reflected in personal and civic insecurities compounded by cultural modes of consumption. This cultural explanation, when Japan was compared to what were considered 'developed countries', went beyond the economic, though, pointing to broader problems of democratic accountability and individual independence and the power and influence of the United States. The Japanese had been rendered culturally insecure by such rapid alterations to their country's economy. Although the government claimed Japan was becoming like Europe, in reality that day was still very far away. Japan was closer to Europe's past than its present, and the deep gulf between the two was clear. By going abroad and gaining experience of the world Hayashi hoped that Japanese women might change 'their thinking, their learning of housework, their means of putting themselves in society', at the same time as they became global people.[66]

Hayashi's trip of discovery, then, was about building a Japanese identity which could become part of a global modernity. That would help those Japanese lucky enough to be able to travel to Europe and understand the importance of democracy and civil society, but also the value of a deep culture that could go beyond the wasteful model of US consumerism. The readers of *Fujin Kōron* were urged to view the opening up of the country as an opportunity for reflection and cultural critique, setting themselves and their ideas of Japan into a global modernity that was Western but not necessarily American. *Shūkan Heibon* and *Heibon Punch* celebrated the new opportunities for travel and presented the world as a place of excitement, in which young Japanese people could take advantage of their new-found freedom to shed their cultural inhibitions and live as a 'human being'. As the Tokyo Olympics approached in 1964, the debate in the media brought these two perspectives together. The transformation of the everyday lives of the Japanese people through increasing consumerism and the search for a national identity within a global modernity dominated by Western-style 'mass consumer consciousness' merged in the media discourse over the hosting of the Games.

Danger within and without

Taking the previous Olympiad in Rome in 1960 as an example, the Tokyo Olympics became the trigger for large-scale urban improvement. Japan, and particularly Tokyo, was dramatically rebuilt to prepare for the Games, with 97.25 per cent of the budget spent on urban expansion and the improvement of infrastructure.[67] In January 1964, nearly ten months before the start of the event, the *Asahi Graph* published images and commentary on the building work being carried out in Tokyo. The journal boasted that the Tokyo Olympiad would be 'the first celebration of beauty and power in the East, adorned with the unique ideas of Japan and supported by world class civil engineering'.[68]

A spectacular demonstration that Japan had achieved the standards of more economically advanced countries, the *Asahi* focused on those buildings that would host Olympic events. The 'postwar' was certainly over.[69] For novelist and cultural critic Yasuoka Shōtarō, the Tokyo Games brought a certain amount of peace to the hearts of the Japanese after the worries of the immediate postwar period. Critic Etō Jun watched an opening ceremony that 'showed a Japan which could at last take its place in the world'.[70] Peace-loving and democratic, the Japan on display in 1964 had also thoroughly abandoned the militaristic and feudal tendencies of the 1930s and 1940s and could now be completely reintegrated into international society.[71]

Less than twenty years after the end of the war, the Games also projected an image of a rebuilt, modern country centred on Tokyo, a capital city which offered up an example of modernization to be emulated by other countries in Asia. The Tokyo Olympics affirmed Japan's existence in the world, and confirmed for the Japanese people their identity within a world of nations. As the *Asahi Graph* recalled a few weeks after the closing ceremony: 'The children of Tokyo had (the fact of) their existence among the many countries of the world burned into their eyes, and the visitors experienced first-hand the heart and energy of the Japanese people (*Nihonjin*). It was a truly precious month'.[72]

Regarding the Tokyo Olympiad, Christian Tagsold has argued that 'symbolic politics and the burden of history called for image management not simply in order to enhance marketing opportunities but to reconstruct national identities'.[73] Yet it was the prospect of new spaces and places of consumption that excited the young readers of *Shūkan Heibon* and *Heibon Punch* but troubled the older, more middle-class readers of the housewife magazines and high-brow journals. A high-speed monorail had been constructed to link the centre of Tokyo with the country's busiest airport, Haneda. New roads and highways, new subway lines and the stadiums and facilities which would be used to host the games were impressive examples of the dream modern city. The freedom to shed their consciousness as Japanese and become global people was now even easier to achieve. In the popular media, by 1964, the promise of a lifestyle of consumption and leisure came together with the emphasis on a global modernity epitomized by Tokyo.

Reconstructing national identity in this context was about the banality of an everyday life that played out in the spaces and places of consumption. The freedom offered by international and national travel was now embedded in the process of individual consumption. Haneda International Airport was only thirty minutes away from the centre of Tokyo, thanks to a fantastic new highway. The nature of these changes and their basis in consumer culture were underlined by the fact that while around 50,000 people per day visited the airport itself, 20,000 of them were there purely to see the airport. For these tourists there was a flight simulator, which gave the experience of 'really flying in an aeroplane'. At four to five degrees cooler than the city, the airport was a great place to take in the view and the leisure mood was epitomized by a rooftop beer garden where, according to Mr Nakazawa of the airport building management company, the beer drunk in the evening while gazing at the amazing illuminations of the airport 'tasted completely different'. With the opening in September of the high-speed monorail, it would be possible to travel from Haneda airport to the city of Hamamatsu non-stop in just fifteen minutes. At Hamamatsu a heliport was planned next to the monorail station, a bus terminal would be built and eventually the monorail would be extended to Shimbashi.[74]

Domestically the opportunities to travel, to experience culture and excitement were just as enticing. In July 1964, the world's fastest rail network was unveiled. Capable of carrying people from Tokyo to Osaka in just three hours, the Shinkansen would begin passenger services right before the beginning of the games in October. As a sign of the rapid development of the country, this was a feat of engineering which would allow the intrepid Japanese office lady to skip work for the day, visit her boyfriend in Kyoto for lunch, after that visit some temples and easily return home by 8.30 pm, then 'with a look of innocence, give the excuse of overtime work before joining in her sister's birthday party'.[75] The changes above ground were impressive, but of greater interest to the magazine's young and single readers may have been the fact that Ginza would see a great new underground 'date spot'. Once the underground lines and the marble shopping arcades were finished, amorous young couples would be able to 'see a film in Hibiya and then enjoy shopping in Ginza'. For those who wanted to soak up just 'a smidgen' of the 'gorgeous atmosphere' at the airport, there was a hotel on the third floor of the international departures lounge which could be reached (rooms for two costing 2,800 yen for three hours!) via the escalator in the lounge.[76] The shrinking of the country through the development of world-leading Japanese technology made travelling around the country much easier. At the same time, the possibility of individual freedom and the enticement of new leisure spaces and places of consumption threatened the prospect of the young and impressionable working-class women being taken advantage of.

Writing in *Fujin Kōron* in August 1964, Furugaki Tetsurō described the coming games as a national ordeal which Japan, and particularly Japanese women, would have to pass successfully. All over the world the mood set by the Tokyo Olympics was overwhelming. In France, the United States and Europe, newspapers, radio and television programmes were full of special editions about Tokyo, and Japanese cuisine, dance cabaret and restaurants had become fashionable around the world.[77] According to Furugaki, Tokyo would need to prepare to welcome tourists on honeymoon, celebrating silver wedding anniversaries, or people celebrating retirement and the Japanese people should give them something to remember as a once-in-a-lifetime experience. But the overarching worry was about the reputation of Japan, and 'its position in the world'. The Games themselves were like a school entrance test, the people 'should think our Olympics begin after the closing ceremony'.[78] The trick for Furugaki was to think about how to pass the test while not forgetting that the real work would only begin after the spectacle of the Olympic Games was over. The Games presented a chance for Japan to join the ranks of the advanced countries, but the modernization this entailed was something the country could later come to regret.

Furugaki reminded readers of the eve of 'the opening of the country' 100 years earlier in the Meiji era. In every area of society, politics, economics and manufacturing policies, 'enlightenment and the catchphrase of freedom were put into practice'. At the beginning of the Meiji period, all over Japan, but particularly in Tokyo, hotels, bars and restaurants catering for high-class foreign tourists changed the nature of the country's economy and brought Westernization. The fear was that the transformation of the country in 1964 would also entail the loss of something essential to Japan. Tokyo had been 'painted with the brush of the Olympics', a mistake Paris and London had avoided. The traditional Japanese culture, which would have been of interest to the huge number of tourists arriving in Japan, had gone. People had not only visited London and Paris to experience the sport; they had also taken in the culture and history of the respective cities. Like Hayashi Shūji, Furugaki saw in Europe the preservation of traditional culture in the face of the rapid development of a wasteful mass consumer culture that Japan had been unable to control. In Tokyo, sport and fashion had completely taken over. Where was the uniqueness of old Japan, or even of modern Japanese culture and tradition? 'The foreign visitors, coming from one hundred and ten countries have different languages, customs, laws, history and traditions we can't reflect them all. But *they* will all want to know about our country.'[79]

If Hayashi Shūji hoped Japanese women would go out into the world to learn how to live better and think about the wastefulness of a consumer culture taken from the United States, Furugaki hoped that they would save 'traditional Japan' from disappearing. In his opinion it was Japanese women who preserved traditional Japanese virtue. For those foreigners seeking to learn about Japan it would be easier for them to understand Japanese culture through its women.[80] Japanese women were traditionally well-mannered and had the tendency, more than men, to reflect on their weak points. The housewives and young women of Japan could explain Japanese cuisine, art, music and culture to the world. Without the familiarity of home-produced goods, services, language and even a recognizable alphabet, foreign guests would feel lost as soon as they stepped from their hotel rooms, yet at some point during their stay they would 'want to eat tasty Japanese food which is close at hand.' However, 'without a Japanese person to tell them the best place to go they will be at a loss.'[81]

In the same journal, several commentators were a little worried about the idea of thousands of foreign men learning about Japanese culture from its 'meek, well mannered, and beautiful women.' In an article entitled 'Dangerous Foreigners,' Fujiwara Yoshie offered her readers much needed 'advice on how to skilfully get along with foreign men.'[82] She agreed that many foreigners were not only coming to see the Olympic Games. 'Foreigners are thronging. Fujisan can be seen, drunks can be seen and these two things are world famous. But this time one more thing which I think tourists will be particularly interested in is young Japanese women.' It was often argued that Japanese women had become stronger since the end of the war. Nevertheless, Fujiwara pointed out, 'our women, as well as still possessing a womanly side, have a character which gives them a double advantage over women of other countries.' There was no room for doubt in Fujiwara's mind that 'for men, Japanese women are number one for charm'. This was not a particularly difficult position to achieve according to the author because, unfortunately, in 'foreign countries, even beautiful daughters (young ladies) of 18 or 20 gradually become old, and at around 40 or 50 most of them, just like a tank, become fatter and fatter'. This was also a problem for Japanese women whose partners were foreigners, because 'if their partner is a foreigner, (*gaijin*) they develop in the same way'.[83]

The increasing visibility of young, single women on the streets of Japan in the spaces and places of consumption that would greet the foreign tourists was clearly a problem for Fujiwara. The attitude of these charming and attractive Japanese women towards foreign men was also a big problem, made all the more serious by the popular media and its focus on entertainment and popular culture. According to Fujiwara, it was as if the young women 'have an open country policy to foreign men, and as with the popular famous actors, they are all unfortunately admired as being tall and handsome. How will they handle it when tens of thousands of these foreign men descend on Japan? It gives me indigestion to think about it'.[84] The idea, raised by Furugaki, that something unique to Japan would be lost with the coming of the Olympics, and particularly through the reality of foreigners visiting the country in pursuit of an ideal of Eastern Beauty, was for Fujiwara literally embodied by the danger faced by young Japanese women, given the flood of foreign men who would be arriving in the country, and their new found freedom in a society geared towards popular consumption.

Nevertheless, despite the fact that as the Olympics approached many voices could be heard worrying about Japanese women, Fujiwara herself, regardless of the ample attractions and charms of the nation's womanhood, not to mention their open-arms policy towards foreigners, confessed to being confident that the women of Japan would cope. After defeat in the war, contact with foreigners had increased and Japanese people were much more used to it. Anyway, she did not think 'that the visitors having to spend lots of money coming from far away will be bad people'. The high cost of the airfare from Europe would settle Fujiwara's indigestion by keeping away those 'bad' foreign men with a curiosity in Japanese women. 'Western' men posed less of a problem anyway. At the end of the day 'if we have to be cautious, it is those close to us from Southeast Asia isn't it? After all, the travel cost is cheap and their attitudes are well known'.[85] Japan had as much, if not more, to fear from Asia as from the West.

Unlike Furugaki, Fujiwara saw the country's traditional customs as part of the problem. In addition to the natural attractiveness of Japanese women, Fujiwara noted that Japan had certain customs which demanded that Japanese women should put their heart into whatever men wanted. 'As soon as a man takes out a cigarette they offer him a light, they put sugar in his coffee, help him on with his jacket, give a yukata to a man wearing only underwear.' Foreign men, even the married or attached ones, would be surprised by these actions and it would be only natural that they would think, 'this woman is for sale'.[86] Worrying that she may be stereotyping foreign men a little too much, or perhaps not enough, Fujiwara felt it necessary to point out that even among Western European men, there were big differences. The 'gentleman' type was to be found in England and America; such men were full of tact and would wait till they passed to turn around and sneak a glance. It was the 'Latin types' that were the most dangerous. 'Italian, Spanish, South American; (these) are the Latin types that will pursue everywhere no matter how far and absolutely never give up.' They would take any chance to start a conversation, 'Excuse me what is the time? Or do you speak English? Can you tell me how to get to … ? Will you come and drink tea with me? You are beautiful. I really appreciate Japanese women.'[87]

These men always came across as astonishingly kind and courteous to women, mainly because they had been raised since childhood to see women as weak, and for Fujiwara Japanese women were indeed weak, particularly around alcohol. In Western Europe, women could enjoy alcohol, but for Japanese women this was not the case. The problem was that in a nice bar, with some 'mood music and a sweet cocktail, Japanese women could quickly come to believe they were in love'. Their weakness was even worse when it came to going for a drive. 'Just putting them in the passenger seat of a cool car makes them feel like a queen.' The 'Latin type' in particular would then try to tempt you to stay overnight. 'It's too late to return, let's stay one night and I will take you back first thing in the morning'. At this point Fujiwara advised readers to call home or ask for a taxi.[88]

In the same 'Olympic special' as Fujiwara's article, thirty people 'from different walks of life' talked to the magazine about their worries about the coming of the Olympic Games. Critic Ishigaki Ayako was, like Fujiwara Yoshie, worried about the inability of Japanese people – particularly young women – to say no. She claimed that when spoken to by men, Japanese young women would often simply offer a coy smile and whatever the question this reaction would probably be taken to mean yes by foreign men. Japanese people needed to be able to say 'no'. Ambiguity and evasion was not the best way to endear foreigners to Japan.[89] Novelist Hirabayashi Taiko was as worried as Fujiwara about the bad foreigners who would arrive in the country looking to deceive Japanese young women. For her, another aspect of the problem was that Japanese men lacked etiquette towards Japanese women. Foreign men, on the other hand, were good at hiding their inner feelings and putting on appearances.[90] They could not be trusted. The 'Japanese woman', unable to see the threat, needed to be protected. The purity of all Japanese women was at stake.

Yet it was not simply that all foreign men were dangerous and all Japanese women needed to be protected. The real danger for those writing in the middle-class magazines such as *Fujin Kōron* had more to do with the need to control the behaviour of those readers of magazines such as *Shūkan Heibon*, who were young, single, working women and frequented the shopping centres and entertainment districts where visitors from all over the world would be found. As Paul Droubie has pointed out, the leaflets distributed to such women, hotel staff and other service industry workers, by the Tokyo Metropolitan government regarding the dangers of sexually transmitted diseases, were brushed off as a revival of the 'Black ships danger'.[91] For the intellectuals, as in the Meiji period, both Japanese women and Japanese culture were threatened by the arrival of foreigners and the changes wrought on the country in preparation for the Olympics. Furugaki saw purity threatened, and looked back to the Meiji period when the threat of Westernization also entailed the loss of traditional culture. The rapid modernization of the high-speed growth era and the welcoming of the world to Tokyo posed the same threat. The shrinking of the world and the increasing freedom apparently offered by consumer society posed serious danger. These fears were grounded in the emergence of a class of young, female workers literally buying into the national ideal of economic development through the promotion of mass consumerism.

Of course, the weekly magazine *Shūkan Heibon*, read by those younger and mainly single women, was a little less worried about the problems posed by foreign men. Talking to foreigners was actually a great way to gain knowledge about the world. The magazine even encouraged its readers to actively seek out foreigners to speak to. 'If you have a chance to have a conversation with a foreigner, or if you optimistically make your own opportunity to get acquainted with a foreigner, through these exchanges young women can get the knowledge of the real world that they need.' The readers should not complain that they lacked the opportunity to talk to foreigners – everybody would have the chance. Japanese people should have will and pride, 'and warmly welcome our guests from afar'.[92] The magazine urged its readers to approach lost foreign tourists at train stations or department stores. They could even fulfil Furugaki's wish and promote 'traditional Japanese culture' because, 'when visiting temples, explaining things about Japan' would make the tourists very happy.

As an American teacher at the Patricia Charm School pointed out, it was usually male students and young businessmen who talked to foreigners. Young women may feel embarrassed, but they should find the courage to strike up a conversation. Questions such as 'How do you like this country?' and 'Is it your first visit to this country?' as well as 'How do you like the food here?' would be the ideal way to break the ice. However, it was important to avoid being ambiguous in conversation with these foreign visitors. According to Mizawa-san, a tour guide for foreign tourists, being ambiguous was the biggest mistake. When you meet foreigners, 'if you say yes or no clearly there should be no excuse for misunderstanding'. Lynda Beech, possibly the most famous American woman in Japan in the mid-1960s, cautioned readers on how to dress. Fluent in Japanese and known to millions as the star of the late 1950s and early 1960s TV hit *Blue Eyes Tokyo Diary*, in which she played an inept American woman living in Tokyo, Beech offered readers the valuable insight of a 'Western' woman.[93] She informed readers that if women wore a low cut dress with lots of jewellery in the morning they would be thought of as cheap. She also advised caution when dealing with foreign men, and warned readers against going anywhere on a date where there would be no other people present. Not because foreign men were any different from Japanese men though, after all, 'If you walk together in the park late at night it's the same danger as walking with a Japanese man … when you go out to the cinema there will be no mistakes.'[94]

A good example of how to stay safe while meeting foreigners was set by Imamura Reiko (22), who worked for a trading company. At work she knew one foreign gentleman who was 'very gentlemanly and very kind', nevertheless whenever she met him in the evenings outside of work she always made sure to invite along another female friend. Readers needed to bear in mind that foreign men were great at offering compliments and Japanese women must avoid being taken in by them. 'Foreigners will constantly flatter you with phrases like "your eyes are beautiful, your hair is fantastic", indeed many foreign men considered it rude not to compliment a woman'. An anonymous, presumably Japanese man, referred to only as A-shi (29), who had experience of living in a foreign country working for a trading company, echoed Fujiwara's fears over the 'open door policy' of Japanese women towards foreign men stating that 'because there are not many foreigners in Japan they are valued highly and there are many women who want to become good at dating foreigners (*gaijin*)'. Japanese women had to remember that there were 'many awful *gaijin* with no education'. A-shi feared that Japanese women who were not used to being 'spoken to sweetly will be excited by this, won't they?' Nevertheless, the readers of *Shūkan Heibon* had far less to fear than those of *Fujin Kōron*, as the article asked its readers: 'are they bad foreigners? That depends on your behaviour'.[95]

The young men of Tokyo, on the other hand, could look forward to the adventures offered by a Tokyo night scene that had become internationalized. In September 1964, *Heibon Punch* featured an article which, under a photo of a smiling young blonde woman dining with two Japanese men, explained that dating 'beautiful blondes' was no longer just a dream. Tokyo was a cosmopolitan city and the opportunities for young Japanese men to 'associate' with beautiful foreign women had rapidly increased. After the appearance of Ai George at Carnegie Hall and the success of Astro Boy in the United States, the increasing number of flights between the United States and Japan brought an influx of stewardesses who, coming to Japan more than ten times a year 'probably lose the normal, everyday sense of virtue'. Women from all over the world were in Tokyo and the possibilities for dating them were huge.

According to one American woman, 'Japanese men may be very shy … nobody has asked me for a date. I wonder whether I am attractive or not …'[96] As the debate in *Fujin Kōron* made clear, it was natural etiquette for foreign men to ask women on a date. Japanese men needed to pluck up the courage to do the same. As one American stewardess put it, 'amongst our friends there are very few Japanese men. I have been married for two years already, but my body is my body and I want to enjoy adventures. Yet I feel bored as soon as I touch down at Haneda … I always wonder is there nothing more to do than go shopping in the department stores, go to my hotel room and read … Japan is the most boring place … I wonder why …' The availability and sexualization of foreign women went hand in hand with the fears over predatory foreign men and the weakness of Japanese women. Of course, it was not only the showgirls and the airhostesses that provided the aspiring young man about town with the opportunity for fun with a foreign lady. The rise in tourists offered the perfect chance to 'catch a foreigner' and waiting around the hotels would pay dividends in that respect. Like the female readers of *Shūkan Heibon*, *Heibon Punch* readers were encouraged to explain 'traditional culture'. Young female tourists would, according to the magazine, be very grateful for anyone offering information on the customs of Japan, explaining the rules of Judo and following up with 'how about a dinner tonight?' was sure to end in success. As a page from 'P Hotel' in Akasaka put it, 'if you are looking for a one night stand there are many housewives in tour groups'.[97] These older ladies were usually attracted to the luggage-carrying bell boy though. The groups of young athletes about to descend on Tokyo also made great targets.[98]

While middle-class readers were urged to see young Japanese women as weak and under threat, young, working female readers of *Shūkan Heibon* were encouraged to associate with the tourists coming to Tokyo and take responsibility for their own actions and safety. The Tokyo Metropolitan Welfare Division's 1964 *Handbook for Young Women* warned of the dangers posed by foreign men, and this became a recurring theme in the mass media.[99] But the focus in *Shūkan Heibon* was on how to date a foreigner, and emphasized the differences between Japanese men and foreign ones. Foreign men were always polite and knew how to 'act like a gentleman'. While the more middle-class journals and magazines fretted over the threat, it was not their readers, the middle-class housewives of *Fujin Kōron*, for example, who were threatened. They knew better.

Yet, for young, increasingly well-off, single, working women, and men, the Olympics was presented as an opportunity to play a role in a global modernity that connected individual freedom to mass consumerism, travel and leisure time. Readers of *Shūkan Heibon* would no doubt have responded in the same way to the articles by Furugaki and the opinions of Fujiwara et al., as the Tokyo hotel worker responded to the Tokyo government's handbook. The obsession with the experience and safety of Japanese women during the games was a metaphor for the nation as a whole, but the mixed reactions to the coming of large numbers of foreign tourists and the danger they posed to Japanese women also reflected the differing experiences of consumer culture and the meaning of nation, and the connection of the individual to it, in everyday life.

Conclusion

'As we move towards a more open system our lifestyles are undergoing big changes',[100] declared *Fujin Kōron* in July 1964. Since the late 1950s, there had been dramatic changes in the large department stores, wrote Kanto Gakuen professor Daimon Kazuki. The imported goods being sold were becoming more luxurious and even in small shops it was common to see shelves packed with foreign-made goods. Imports had been steadily increasing, and compared with 1959, golf goods, toys, toothbrushes and instant coffee had increased by between forty and sixty times. Imports of cigarette lighters had risen 300 times, and mechanical pencils 100 times. Imported goods were 'gradually beginning to widen their presence in the everyday life of the Japanese people (*nihonjin no seikatsu*)'. With the help of a survey commissioned by the magazine which asked 200 people to rate the quality of thirty-three different items, Daimon aimed to 'get a true sense of the value of foreign made and domestically produced goods' because 'we are at a stage where we have to decide which is more important – the price or the quality?'[101]

The camera was rated number one among domestically produced goods, and the razor number one among foreign-made goods. Seventy-two versus ten of the respondents agreed that Japanese cameras were well made and given that two-thirds of the stock of the number one US camera retailer, Willoughby's, was produced in Japan this was understandable. Thanks in part to the advent of hire purchase and the desire for fashionable cheap clothes among young single women in the cities, Japanese-made sewing machines had overtaken US products as the most preferred among housewives. Indeed the sewing machine was fast becoming 'number one among presents bought by tourists coming to Japan'. The problem with this, as far as Daimon was concerned, was the expense. For the well off, this increasing consumerism was no problem at all, but there was no guarantee that this would be open to all.[102]

In a round-table debate hosted by Hayashi Shūji in early 1964 in *Fujin Kōron*, Hayashi admitted to his belief that without Ikeda's policy of separating politics and economics there would have been no improvement in the livelihood of the Japanese people (*kokumin seikatsu*). But he also pointed out that rising prices were not necessarily matched by rising wages, and, according to Yamamoto Susumu of the *Economist*, it was the middle classes, married salarymen with children, who were the worst affected by the promotion of consumption.[103] A shortage of labour in Japan meant that starting wages for young Japanese workers were rising rapidly and that the rise in income had a knock-on effect on the cost of living for everybody. This meant that, in real terms, the wages of public officials and salarymen were declining. Ultimately, the policies of economic growth were leading to an increase in wages for factory workers who tended to be younger and generally not from middle-class backgrounds.[104]

This development was creating a class of young consumers with different ideas, outlooks and cultural orientation from the more traditional university-educated middle classes. With the growing emphasis on consumption in the popular media, *Shūkan Heibon* and *Heibon Punch* exemplified a youth culture which sought to reject the structured nature of Japanese society, yet struggled to escape the everyday life of consumer society. In many ways, being closely tied to American military and economic power, the rise of consumerism deliberately pursued by Ikeda, was, as Guy Yasko has noted, simply one more assault on popular sovereignty.[105] Yet, by the time of the 1964 Tokyo Olympics, the promotion of consumer society formed the basis of a depoliticized cultural nationalism that could appeal, through the growing popular media, to a younger generation of workers and students experiencing the alienation of life in the cities. The lifestyles on offer in these magazines became Japanese even as, indeed perhaps because, they appeared to epitomize a global modernity that Japan had finally taken its place within.

4

The Contradictions of Consumer Society

Isn't it hard to find a reason to be angry in Japan today ... ? If Japan's young writers are writing angry novels it is simply because anger has become a commodity.

Ooya Soichi[1]

Peace and prosperity

In 1946, Matsushita Konnosuke set up the PHP (Peace and Happiness through Prosperity) foundation to 'bring peace and fulfilment to human society by ensuring both material and spiritual abundance'. As a businessman, he believed it was his duty 'to ensure products were available to consumers as readily as running water'.[2] Just twenty years later they were, and in *Heibon Punch*'s fourth anniversary publication of 26 August 1968, Matsushita won fourth place in a reader's poll to find 'Mr International'. Founder of the electronics company which traded under the brand name National, he signified the importance of consumer society to the magazine's young readers. Having built up a successful Japanese electronics empire and almost singlehandedly created 'Japanese' products, Matsushita's attraction for readers of the magazine was explicitly nationalistic, although National did provide 2.3 million Yen worth of goods to be dished out in a prize draw to 1,609 of the readers who cast their vote. These 'National Young man products' included a luxury nine-piece set including a stereo, bicycle, transistor television, car stereo, portable television, tape recorder, transistor radio, as well as a trouser press for the lucky winner nineteen-year-old Yamada-san from Kyoto. Five hundred winners received a *Heibon Punch* tiepin and 1,000 a *Heibon Punch* handkerchief. Nevertheless, according to the magazine, Matsushita was essential to the times because of his vast business empire, which astonished those members of the economic intelligentsia who 'insisted on the economic assistance of an old power like America'.[3]

Just two years earlier in 1966, novelist and anti-war activist Oda Makoto had sensed a change in the attitude of young Japanese towards nationalism since the ANPO protests of 1960. Back during the height of the anti-treaty protests, in answer to the question 'what do you think about Japan?' Oda claimed that maybe one out of ten would reply 'Japan is great'. When asked the more serious question of whether they would give their lives to protect the country if it was invaded, most would simply laugh and say that they would run. Even those who claimed to love their country would have had difficulty understanding the concept of protecting it according to Oda. Six years later, when asked the same question, Oda predicted that 80 per cent would answer 'Japan is great'. Asked whether they would give their lives to protect the country they now answered 'as if it were self-evident'. Yet they could not explain why they were prepared to give up their lives for Japan, or what it was about the country that they would want to protect. He referred to this sentiment as 'irresponsible nationalism' (*musekinin na nashonarizumu*) and blamed it on the Tokyo Olympics.[4]

As seen in the previous chapter, through the media discourse the Olympics tied the experience of everyday life to a new global modernity based around the pursuit of individual freedom through consumption. The coming of the Olympics allowed for the celebration of a Japan which had returned to the world stage diplomatically and culturally, and at the same time an increasing culture of individual consumption could be seen as part of a global modernity reinforced in the media by images of the foreign visitors populating the new spaces of entertainment and consumption that had sprung up across the cities since the late 1950s. The new kind of nationalism becoming apparent to Oda by 1966 was intimately tied to the growth of this consumer society, and appeared as a fundamental part of a postwar transformation of values dependent on, and reflected in, the Cold War–free world rhetoric of international power politics. By this point, those critical of the rise of the consumer as king in Japan had shifted their attention to the apparent alienation brought about by the increasing rationalization of politics and daily life. Students and intellectuals sought to understand individual and national subjectivity within the matrix of the everyday even as, thanks to high-speed economic growth, the folkways of the major Japanese cities were being paved and, by the mid-1960s, even the ethnographic populism of Yanagita Kunio literally and figuratively spoke for consumerism.[5] Their quest for authenticity was, as Marilyn Ivy has pointed out, caught up in the very historical conditions they hoped to escape.[6]

The results of the 1968 'Mr International' poll emphasized the centrality of the Vietnam War to the everyday lives of *Heibon Punch*'s readers. French president Charles De Gaulle was the overwhelming victor with 52,833 votes. David Condè, a special correspondent for the political magazine *Canadian Forum*, praised his role in standing up for the sovereignty and determination of small countries such as 'France, Vietnam and Japan' in their partnership with the powerful United States. 'As a champion of national independence he will probably continue to be a hero fighting for real independence'.[7] After all, the general 'carried the spirit of national independence (*minzoku dokuritsu*)' in an international arena dominated by the United States – a sentiment backed up by the third place finish of Ho Chi Minh. This chapter will show how the Vietnam War's connection to consumer culture and rapid economic growth in Japan was inseparable from the nature of the medium of the popular magazine. It not only allowed for what Jean Baudrillard describes as the 'disarticulation of the real into successive equivalent signs … the miraculous transition from Vietnam to variety, on the basis of a total abstraction of both'.[8] In Japan, in the popular media, the war also worked to stitch together individual experience of the everyday and the national and international framework of postwar imperialism by making explicit the connection between consumer society and high-speed economic growth.

The chapter will follow on from the discussion in the previous chapter by showing how the reintegration of national symbols went beyond the political and diplomatic concerns of the hosting of the Olympics. The flag and the national anthem became increasingly visible in the lives of young Japanese, but not in direct connection to the state. It was in the spaces and places of entertainment and consumption, within the consumer culture that represented individual freedom and democratic expression, that these divisive national symbols were reintegrated. At the same time, the Vietnam War revealed the ambiguity inherent in the division between internal and external at the level of both individual and nation, because the idea of a national identity separated from the experience of everyday life gradually became more difficult to sustain. While Vietnam apparently offered an external, 'international' example of a small country standing up for its national independence against the power and influence of the United States, and Matsushita Konnosuke offered the economic equivalent for Japan, in *Heibon Punch*, Mishima Yukio, second place in the 'Mr International' competition, offered an example to those searching for individual independence by challenging the normality of an increasingly standardized society. Mishima and the student protesters who took to the streets in the mid–late 1960s, sought to reconcile the external elements of national subjectivity with the internal dilemmas thrown up by rapid social and economic change.[9]

At the time of *Heibon Punch*'s search for 'Mr International', the contradictions inherent in the country's postwar economic growth were driving much of the discourse in the popular media. The student and anti-war protests were inseparable from the international context of the late 1960s, but intimately tied to the individual experience of everyday life. At the same time, the issue of Japan's relations with the rest of Asia and the domestic and international problems epitomized by the status of Okinawa created a discourse that stitched together that experience with the complex and ambiguous relationship between the national and the international in the context of the promotion of consumer society.

'National symbols'

The emphasis on the consumer as king since the start of the 1960s came to encompass the concerns of the individual, the national and the international by the time of the Tokyo Olympics. The ambiguous relationship between individual subjectivity, national identity and the international was brought to the fore in the media discourse over the status of the traditionally national symbols of the flag and anthem. On 4 January 1964, just before a televised world championship boxing match, the popular Japanese singer Ai George sang *Kimigayo* live. The song was not legally recognized as the national anthem and in the run-up to the Olympic Games its use sparked a debate in the popular media that raised important historical issues and polarized opinion. This debate over national symbols made evident a generational divide centred on issues of war and defeat, but the report of Ai George's performance of *Kimigayo*, in January 1964, raised these deeply political and historical issues within the boundaries of a popular culture that had emerged through the development of a consumer society intimately connected to the global concerns of the Cold War.

According to *Shūkan Heibon*, Ai's rendition deeply impressed the entire audience. His performance of the song was not broadcast live on television, but it was well-known that in September 1963, at the beginning of a flyweight title match, the soon-to-be-golden disc recipient Sakamoto Kyū did sing *Kimigayo* live on Japanese television. The song was controversial, yet, to many young people, it was almost unknown. In the 1950s, with little experience of either the song or the flag, many schoolchildren believed both the *Hinomaru* and *Kimigayo* to be the flag and song of the national television broadcaster NHK.[10] Visiting his grandfather's house in Nagano at New Year, one Tokyo primary school student explained that, when *Kimigayo* was played on the television, his grandfather corrected his sitting position and listened intently. 'When I asked "what's wrong?" he replied "it's the Japanese national anthem, you have to listen to it sitting in the seiza style!" I asked again, "Is Kimigayo like a sutra?"'[11] The connection to religious observance neatly encapsulated the political nature and historical legacies of political symbols of nation in the postwar period. Nevertheless, at the start of the year of the Tokyo Olympics, Ai George believed that the value of *Kimigayo* was increasing and it was for this reason that he sang it. 'On January 4th, I turned down all other New Year work in order to sing that song. That's how much effort I put into singing it'.[12]

At the start of the US Occupation in 1945, around the time most of Ai George's fans would have been born, the issue of the future status of the Japanese flag and national anthem was unclear. Immediately after the surrender, there were reports of American servicemen taking down the flag as they secured the mainland and, unsurprisingly, these reports led many to believe the anthem and the flag would be banned.[13] Defeat meant that the symbolic representation of a nation that was explicitly connected to the Japanese state, connected to war and defeat, needed to be redefined. Yet, rather than enforcing an outright ban on the flying of the *Hinomaru* or the singing of *Kimigayo*, Occupation authorities took a more ambivalent approach. SCAP, particularly MacArthur, had little problem allowing the flying of the flag or the singing of the anthem on certain occasions. In 1949, SCAP stated that it had no issue with the flying of the flag anywhere within the limits of Japanese territory.[14] In his New Year message to the Japanese people, General MacArthur made clear his permission for all groups in society to use the flag 'without limit'. At the same time, he also made it clear that the *Hinomaru* would stand for international peace and cooperation.[15]

It has been claimed that the publically redesigned flag unveiled in 1964 was a product of democracy and internationalism.[16] For young people born after the war, the reality was a little more ambiguous. In preparation for the Olympic Games in 1964, there was a competition to redesign the flag, but this ultimately only amounted to adjusting the size of the sun disc and the parameters of the flag itself. As with the promotion of consumer society, the symbolic promotion of democracy and internationalism by the Japanese state was premised on a discourse developed under the US Occupation and built upon as the Cold War in East Asia developed. In his notes on the new Japanese constitution, General Douglas MacArthur had stated his hope that the Japanese flag would symbolize 'the coming of a new era of permanent peace based on individual freedom, dignity, magnanimity, and justice …'[17] MacArthur's hope was, like those involved in planning the hosting of the Olympic Games, that the flag would serve to integrate Japan into the international system of nation states. It would be a symbol of the democratic and peace-loving nation created by the reforms of the US Occupation.

According to an *Asahi* newspaper survey, 73 per cent of those surveyed in 1950 admitted to having a flag at home, but, of those, only 30 per cent took the flag out on festival days. The newspaper claimed that the destruction caused by the heavy bombing of urban areas during the war was one reason for the disappearance of the *Hinomaru*. Not only did many people no longer possess a flag, they did not even possess a home from which to fly it![18] MacArthur's statement made clear that, after 1945, the symbolic meaning of the Japanese flag would change. Rather than the militaristic Emperor system, the flag would have to represent a new, democratic and peaceful Japan. Throughout the 1950s, in order for these new meanings to become convincing for the Japanese people, the flag would need to assume greater prominence in their everyday lives. With the growth of the popular media and the emergence of television, by 1964, it had.

The status and desirability of the 'national anthem' *Kimigayo* also created debate and discussion. According to the *Asahi*, many Japanese believed *Kimigayo* did not 'match the new era' and saw no reason why the song could not be changed. For Shimizu Ikutaro, the song was based on an old way of thinking and was 'out of keeping with the times'.[19] Early in 1951, the *Yomiuri* newspaper asked whether it would be better to write a new national anthem. Of the readers polled, 364 thought the anthem should be kept, while 290 believed it should be abolished. For those in favour of keeping it, *Kimigayo* was 'already merged into the feelings of daily life' and, in the context of 'a democratic Japan under the symbolic Emperor', they saw no contradiction. For those on the opposite side of the debate, the anthem was nothing more than 'barefaced praise of feudalism'.[20] The Japanese government followed MacArthur's advice and attempted to increase the public profile of both the flag and anthem. *Kimigayo* was played at the end of the NHK broadcast of the signing of the San Francisco Peace Treaty, and the flag was shown while the anthem played to mark the first television broadcast in September 1953.

Throughout the 1950s, especially with the growth in access to television, people became used to seeing the flag in everyday life.[21] Still, with the awarding of the Olympic Games to Tokyo in 1959, the fact that there was no legal basis for the *Hinomaru* as the Japanese flag, and the problem of whether *Nihon* or *Nippon* was the correct way of referring to the host country, brought the question of national symbols to the fore in the popular media. Fortunately, by 1964, 80 per cent of respondents to one survey claimed to like the song *Kimigayo*, a sentiment Ai George was channelling when he chose to sing the anthem live on television.[22] By 1964, the young consumers of popular magazines like *Heibon Punch* and *Shūkan Heibon* were increasingly encountering these national symbols in the spaces of entertainment and consumption celebrated by the magazines. The 'national anthems' of West Germany and Japan were played before a performance by the Berlin Opera at the opening ceremony of the Nissei Theatre in Tokyo. Similarly, at a performance in Tokyo by the Polish circus, *Kimigayo* was performed before the show began.

Popular culture was helping to re-incorporate both the flag and the anthem into everyday life. Nevertheless, the reaction and feelings of the people towards both were still very mixed. Ikejima Shimpei, editor-in-chief of monthly magazine *Bungei Shunjun* and of the generation raised before the war, listened to the performance of the song at the Nissei Theatre with what he described as a 'large wave of emotion'. The performance reaffirmed for him 'the excellence of *Kimigayo*'. Thirty-five-year-old Nitta Akio, who came of age during the Occupation period, witnessed the performance at the Polish circus. He described it as a strange feeling and was unsure how to respond. An 'uncomfortable, complicated feeling, should I stand or sit down, I was lost in some feelings of opposition'.[23] According to the magazine, Nitta's opposition was understandable. He was of the generation that had grown up during the war. Having come of age during the Occupation period, the conflicting nature of prewar and postwar state symbols clearly rendered the anthem ambiguous.

For fans of Sumo wrestling, usually of an older generation, the singing of the national anthem was not at all unusual. Starting with the summer *Bashō* of 1952, *Kimigayo* was performed at the closing of the tournament.[24] According to Sumo fan and shop owner Tanaka Eizō, who never missed a *Bashō* and always watched the final day: 'when I am there singing *Kimigayo* I strongly feel that I am Japanese (*Nihonjin*). There really is no other chance to feel this way. That's the reason I always attend the final day of a tournament. The feeling you get is great'.[25] On the other hand, the article pointed out that there was no shortage of people who watched the last day of a tournament on TV and who turned off the TV set when *Kimigayo* began. According to one thirty-six-year-old teacher, 'the idea of a national anthem should be more big-hearted, more optimistic and rhythmical … Also *Kimigayo* brings with it all kinds of unpleasant memories of the war'.[26]

Yasukawa Yoshitsugu saw the flag as an ominous sign. He was born as the war came to an end and was due to attend the coming of age ceremony at the beginning of 1964. 'When the *Hinomaru* is flying in the ceremony hall I can't meekly accept that. I have no particular memories of the war period, but behind that *Hinomaru* I feel the dark hand of the re-emergence of Japanese militarism.' Hata Hiroyasu, on the other hand, who worked in a Chinese restaurant and would attend the same ceremony as Yasukawa, claimed, 'I like the *Hinomaru*. I think it's a great flag. It is only natural that it would be flying in the ceremony hall.'[27] Yasukawa was in the minority of young people, according to *Shūkan Heibon*. Most accepted both the flag and the anthem. The war needed to be forgotten, because, according to one interviewee, 'to reject your national flag and national anthem is stupid'. Japanese people needed to respect Japan. 'If Japanese people (*Nihonjin*) don't respect Japan (*Nihon*), how can we get foreigners to respect Japan?' The Olympics were the perfect moment to educate the young about the importance of national symbols.

Although the Ministry of Education had, in 1958, attempted to incorporate the flag and anthem into compulsory education, the Liberal Democratic Party's Hasegawa Takashi noted it would never be seen in a Japanese classroom in the postwar period. For Hasegawa, the Tokyo Olympics provided the opportunity to make the '*kokumin* love the *Hinomaru*'. 'Young people are gathering from all over the world, different races, overcoming discrimination between different countries deliberately fighting for people's hearts, the flag can do this'. Reiterating the ideological goals of the Olympic movement, Hasegawa saw the flag as a symbol of 'fair play, freshness, and health'. This was a great chance 'to reverse the dark wartime images, and it is with this meaning that I want to see many *Hinomaru* flying at the Olympics'.[28] The official image of Japan portrayed at the Tokyo Olympics was no longer the enemy of a long and brutal war but rather 'a peaceful internationalist'.[29] The Olympic Games provided the perfect opportunity to rehabilitate these divisive symbols. In view of the ideological premise of the Olympic movement, this process would reinforce MacArthur's view of the *Hinomaru* as symbolic of international peace and democratic development.

Yet, just seven years after the Tokyo Olympics, and four after Oda Makoto noted the rise of an irresponsible nationalism among young people in Japan, the integration of national symbols into the consumer society through which they had been rehabilitated was complete. *Heibon Punch* surveyed 500 male and female high school students about their feelings towards the national flag. 'Seeing the *Hinomaru* I feel excitement!' claimed a headline in *Heibon Punch* in the summer of 1971. Posing the question 'What do you think of the *Hinomaru*?' the article reported on the feelings of young people towards the Japanese flag. According to the results, 'tying it to past links with the war and screwing up your face to it' was old-fashioned. Seventy per cent of the students claimed to 'love the *Hinomaru*', while only 20 per cent reported that they did not like it.[30] Regarding the flag's design, when asked what they most associated with it the favourite responses were 'cool', 'passionate', 'symbolic' or 'plain', but only 20 per cent described it as 'worthless'. The article expressed surprise that for a generation who had not known the war at all high school students were surprisingly aware of the flag.

When they were asked about what they associated the *Hinomaru* with, the men and women differed. For both sexes, the number one response was not too surprisingly 'the country's flag', and for men, militarism came second. The third place was taken up by *bentō*, fourth right-wing movements and fifth was given to the emperor. The magazine concluded nonetheless that, among men, 'apart from the innocent desire to eat a *hinomaru bentō*' and even though these high school students 'didn't directly have experience of the war', there was still a strong anti-authority, anti-dictatorship consciousness. Next to this, the women were 'righteously peaceful' in the magazine's opinion, associating the *Hinomaru* secondly with 'the song', third with festivals and a feeling of being on holiday. Perhaps surprisingly, according to the magazine, in the fourth place women associated the flag with war but, 'hopefully unrelated, in fifth place they claimed a feeling of excitement'. Other answers given by the students ranged from pickled plums (*umeboshi*), fried eggs (*medamayaki*), getting on a ship, *momotarō, tokkōtai*, as well as what the magazine described as 'other strange answers'. One student complained that 'for our generation to associate it with militarism and war is sad. But *bentō* and festivals is also deplorable! Why is it not peace or the Yamato spirit which comes out?' The magazine concluded in agreement with Oda that 'depending on how you look at it, it could be said that among high school students a new kind of nationalism (*minzokushugi*)' was being nurtured.[31] This new kind of nationalism combined the emphasis on individual subjectivity in consumer society and the increasingly ambiguous nature of the national and international.

Vietnam to variety

In 1964, Haneda airport had connected the growth of consumer society in Japan to a global modernity based on freedom of consumption, movement and individual freedom. By the end of the decade, the same airport symbolized the contradictions inherent in the pursuit of high-speed economic growth through consumption. In November 1969, the Japanese prime minister Satō Eisaku boarded a Japan Airlines flight to Washington to meet President Nixon for discussions over the renewal of the security treaty. Seven thousand riot police carrying large duralumin shields and quantities of tear gas surrounded the airport, while, across Japan, 50,000 uniformed and plain clothes police officers were deployed to prevent unrest. According to one journalist, the pre-departure mood was 'just like before a civil war'.[32] 'Twenty police boats patrolled nearby rivers, canals, and sections of Tokyo Bay, and helicopters were deployed overhead'. Not far from the airport, 'about 3,000 students from the anti-JCP (Japan Communist Party) factions of *Zengakuren* fought the police with stones and staves near Ōtorii station, resulting in more than 500 injuries and 300 arrests'.[33] Over the night of the 16–17 November, over 1,700 people were taken into police custody, a number which remains the largest arrest in postwar history.[34]

Journalistic talk of civil war may have appeared to be a throwaway remark, but one year previously *Heibon Punch* had reported on running battles in and around Shinjuku station in Tokyo. From 9 pm to midnight on 21 October 1968, students and 'the onlookers following them had the platform at Shinjuku station all to themselves'. Train seats were torn out and set on fire, and glass was broken. The busiest train station in the country was trashed and, in the surrounding streets, cars were set ablaze and a police box was burned down with a Molotov cocktail.[35] Outside the station, before the fighting began, Oda Makoto, the leader of the Anti-Vietnam War movement *Beiheiren*, implored people to 'take a look at the riot police. They are holding truncheons for beating people and are surrounding us. Is this the face of Japan, a supposedly peaceful country?' On this 'anti-war day' when, according to police estimates, 170,000 people attended 270 rallies nationwide, 60,000 commuters 'stood by as riot police stormed the barricades and finally subdued the radicals after midnight with hoses and tear gas'.[36]

In 1969, student radicalism was 'fast becoming institutionalised' across the world. In Japan, Toyomasa Fuse claimed that student radicalism constituted one of the three top priorities in national politics.[37] In addition to the events of 1969 and 1968, violent attempts by students to stop Satō leaving Haneda airport in 1967 had twice brought the issue of violence between protesters and riot police into the mainstream media (the so-called Haneda Incidents). On 8 October, members of *Zengakuren*, the largest association of student groups, forcibly tried to prevent Satō leaving for a trip to Southeast Asia.[38] In the protests one student, Yamazaki Hiroaki, died. One month later, the prime minister was again met with violent protests and, on 11 November, seventy-three-year-old Tadanoshin Yui set himself on fire outside the prime minister's house in protest at the War in Vietnam. Yui believed that the United States was repeating the mistakes Japan itself had made in China during the Second World War. He died the following day, just five minutes before the prime minister's jet took off from Haneda airport for Washington.[39]

Epitomized in Japan by the student movement *Zengakuren*, the *Kaminari* tribe, and through the writings of Ishihara Shintaro and Oe Kenzaburo, the angry young men of the late 1950s were a product of the social and cultural transformations associated with the beginnings of high-growth capitalism, liberal democracy, nuclear tensions and anti-communism.[40] For the *Yomiuri* newspaper, they accepted no responsibility for the direction in which the world was heading; indeed their hope was that by refusing the order of Japanese society and tradition 'something new would be born'.[41] They brought their anger to the fore in literary and intellectual writings which became a commodity in Oya Soichi's terms. For the late 1960s generation, their anger was always already a commodity, thanks to the growth of the popular media. They expressed their frustrations in radical violence, but it was the direction in which Japan and the world were heading that drove them. As Riki Kersten has noted with respect to Todai, in 1968 the students, 'with the prospect of a glorious future ahead of them merely because they had been accepted as students there, began to ask themselves whether they were personally complicit in the inequality and exploitation that pervaded a Japanese society drunk on rapid and high economic growth'.[42]

The *Yomiuri Shimbun* explained that the Haneda incidents were tied up with large-scale opposition protests over 'autonomy for universities, our country's policy towards Vietnam as well as the security problem'.[43] In the view of many young people, state control over national institutions had increased 'the insidious nature of the academic industrial complex'.[44] The increasing competitiveness of education and channelling of students into technical subjects brought about a backlash against the standardization and mechanization of work and education.[45] Certainly, by mid-1969, protesting high school students bluntly bemoaned the fact that 'the Japanese capitalist system underpins high school education'.[46] To combat this, student movements in Japan attempted to assert control over the power structures of everyday life and became 'very much part of an international movement focused on the defence of the self'.[47] Yet, those involved in the protests experienced that self, as well as everyday life and national identity, within the context of the growing mass media and the ambiguities of consumerism. As Jurgen Habermas noted in relation to the student movement in Germany, 'all motivations of a society based on status competition become especially dubious in a social environment in which the young … encounter reality only through the filter of consumer orientations and mass media'.[48]

Between 1967 and 1970, the magazine *Fujin Kōron* carried many articles and special sections attempting to understand or explain the reasons for the violent protests.[49] The role of the Japanese state in the Vietnam War was important, and, in April 1968, Shimada Kazuko, a first year student at Hosei University, explained that the trigger for her involvement was 'making Japan a nuclear armed country and a state which participated in the Vietnam War through the docking of the Enterprise (at Sasebo)'.[50] Yet, in a round-table discussion in the January 1969 issue, the weakening of the division between individual and national subjectivity was apparent. When asked who the enemy was student 'C' explained that it was 'the whole of Imperialism. Some people will say that American imperialism is the enemy. That is not correct. If we say that, it implies there is good and bad imperialism. That's too vague'. 'E' took a more anarchic stance claiming that 'for the people the enemy is everything that oppresses. If I want to do something and somebody is against it they are the enemy'. For 'F' the enemy was rather more abstract, 'for me the enemy is oneself personally'.[51] The role of the state, imperialism and individual responsibility were put forward by different respondents, yet distinguishing between them was becoming increasingly problematic.

Sociologist Sakuta Keiichi of Kyoto University argued that adults needed to try harder to understand Japanese young people. No age group was as introspective as the young. The internal, individual subjectivity of the protesters could not be easily separated from the external issues they addressed through the violence. The discourse of anger and violence in the popular media risked equating their protests with gangsterism by assuming a distinction between external and internal. The apparent heroism of the students, increasingly felt by many people, stemmed from the view of them as brave because they were willing to turn their internal frustrations outwards and take on the power of the state. For most people, in Sakuta's view, internal thought led directly to external action. When students charged at riot police with wooden sticks the students came to see themselves as heroic, because they put their emotions into their actions and sought to change the outside world according to those beliefs.[52]

This type of 'psychological' explanation, the separation between the external, concrete policies and actions of the state and the internal, personal emotions of the students was common in the newspapers. It disgusted Sakuta. The idea that the students were acting heroically by putting their opposition to the state into action, violently expressing what other people could not, led to the protests being seen as 'mob heroism'. Yet, the students needed to be seen as different from the mob to be truly understood. The political issue of the Japanese government's support for the Vietnam War, along with the increasingly competitive education system and its failings, was beside the point. The rapid growth of consumer society and the promotion of individual freedom had led to the breakdown of 'horizontal relations' between people and groups. The nature of the development of postwar capitalism in Japan meant that competition and 'the aim of cooperating only in order to win' had become essential.[53] In Sakuta's view it was this sense of competition that drove the protesters.

The attempt to separate internal and external and the need to violently and bravely clash with the outside world were epitomized for Sakuta by a note written by Yamasaki Hiroaki, the student killed in the protests at Haneda airport. Yamasaki claimed he was 'fundamentally a pacifist' and saw this as a negative thing, explaining that although he was 'a weak human being … all humans are weak'. He believed that, to overcome weakness, the important thing was for human beings to exert themselves, to impose themselves on the world. In Sakuta's view, these sentences could only have been written 'by an introspective person negative about himself'. Such people had interiorized the guilt of society and needed to throw themselves up against that society just to reaffirm their existence. But in terms of the social conditions that influenced them, the Japanese government was far from neutral in Sakuta's opinion. 'The fact that they [the Japanese government] have chosen to stand only on the side of the Americans' was one of the conditions which affected the consciousness of Japanese young people.[54] Capitalism had weakened the bonds of cooperation as it promoted competition, and students and young people had internalized this ethic of competition more than any other section of society. Sakuta urged readers to examine the idea that external problems are external and internal problems are internal.[55] The dilemma of individual subjectivity was increasingly bound up in the media with the national and the international in a society driven by consumerism, but this did not just apply to the young student protester.

'Race war'

A few months after Satō's departure to Washington from the fortress of Haneda airport, the *Asahi Graph* published an article entitled 'Are Japanese People Yellow Whites?' Written by critic Kugai Saburō, the article addressed the massacres being carried out by US forces in Vietnam with the support of the Japanese government. Kugai was worried by the lack of concern in Japan after the massacre at My Lai in March 1968. News of My Lai had begun to emerge in late 1968 and, as someone who travelled widely, frequently to Hanoi, he noticed that more fuss was being made in European countries concerning the actions of American forces in Vietnam.[56] *Time* magazine published graphic photos of the massacre, reports of which had first become known in Britain and then spread across Europe before becoming an explosive political problem in America. Kugai himself had first heard about the massacre in November 1968 when he left Tokyo for one of his trips to Hanoi. He stressed, however, that he got all this information from his time in Hanoi, and not through the Japanese media. In Vietnam, he was often asked why such things were taken up by the Western media leading to large protests, yet the same did not seem to happen in Japan. This led him to pose the question, 'Are we Japanese so insensitive and dehumanised through the process of high speed economic growth that we cannot show a humanitarian response to such an inhuman action?'[57]

By the late 1960s and early 1970s, many Japanese companies were relocating operations to countries which were formerly part of the Japanese Empire. Between 1956 and 1969, Japanese exports to South Vietnam quadrupled, and by 1972 imports of raw materials from South Vietnam had increased seven times over 1958 levels.[58] By 1967, exports to the United States attributable to the war are thought to have increased by $260 million over the previous year, and overall Japanese exports to the United States between 1965 and 1972 grew at an average of 21 per cent per year, partly through normal growth but also because of Vietnam.[59] The Asian Development Bank was established in 1966 to provide funds to non-communist Southeast Asia, and, with the official declaration of the Guam doctrine by President Nixon on 25 July 1969, it became clear that the United States expected Japan to take on a greater financial role in the region.[60] This did not appear to be matched by an increasing sense of responsibility to the people of the region though.

Kugai believed that, compared to Americans and Europeans, the Japanese had more information about such events. The corollary of this, however, was that there was 'no fresh surprise', and, at the same time, 'no protests in response like in Europe and America'.[61] It was partly the Japanese proximity to the war that meant the people did not appear to respond to reports of atrocities. Yet Kugai believed that, as Asians, the Japanese had a duty to protest and make a noise about the crimes of America in Vietnam. After all, the war was 'a war of white America against Asian people … a massacre and genocide against Asian people'. A journalist in Hanoi had rammed this point home to Kugai by pointing out that America tested its new weapons on Asian people first. In Hiroshima it had been nuclear weapons and now, in Vietnam, napalm and chemical weapons. The journalist warned him that, as an Asian, this fact was something Kugai should never forget.

Kugai believed that, while Vietnam was not a racial war, American policy there was 'shot through with the same discrimination which imprisons black people'.[62] In this respect, the Japanese had become more similar to Westerners than to 'the Koreans, Chinese and Vietnamese'. This was more than simply a sense of affinity with the West. As Japan approached the standard of living of the West and gained economic influence in the international arena, finally 'stepping foot in the white pool of African Republics', as Kugai put it, Japanese people had 'come to feel the same racist scorn as Westerners towards Vietnamese and Koreans'.[63] The Japanese who stayed in Phnom Pen, for example, stayed in the same hotels and wore the same clothes as Americans, and they felt the same need to distance themselves from the people of

Southeast Asia.[64] The same scornful attitude was evident in the expression of two Khmer ladies who served him at the ship's offices in Phnom Pen as he made his way back to Japan. They wore French make-up and miniskirts and were fluent in both French and English and, for Kugai, after returning from Hanoi where 'all the women wore *minzoku* uniform' he really felt 'the ladies' elite consciousness'. 'Those expressions said: I am the same as a white person. I am totally different from the poor Southeast Asian people'. As the woman handed him his ticket, Kugai was 'taken by the feeling that, as a Southeast Asian, she was reflecting Japan's position back on itself'.[65] Japanese people had exactly the same consciousness. Their economic superiority allowed them to see themselves as equal to white people, and consequently different from Asians. Affluence trumped ethnicity.

Japan's role in and responsibility for the war in Vietnam was seen by most Japanese people to be due to its enforced position as a base for the American attacks. So for the majority of Japanese people, if Japan was at fault it was because of passive, even unwanted, cooperation with the Americans. But over the previous two decades, the economic links between the countries had increased and the Japanese economy was profiting enormously from the war as exports grew. The leaders of the South Vietnam Freedom Front berated Kugai for this. 'Vietnamese people like Japanese products, but economic aid and skill support helps the puppet power in Saigon. This is a problem because it helps to continue the American invasion'. Japan's economic development was inseparable from the actions of the United States in the eyes of the people of Southeast Asia. In Kugai's opinion, President Nixon's plans for Vietnam were based on Japanese economic development, and all of Southeast Asia knew this. Evidence of Japan's influence in Southeast Asia was everywhere. The foreign minister in Hanoi got straight to the point when he warned Kugai that a 'new Japanese colonialist expansionism' (*shin-shokuminchi shugiteki bōchyōshugi*) was developing.[66]

An old Japanese soldier who had remained in Vietnam after the Second World War and had just recently opened his own Japanese language school backed up this claim noting how, after the 1968 Tet Offensive, the number of students quickly increased. Vietnamese newspapers were full of discussions about how the Japanese economy was developing. Indeed, being taught by Japanese people was really popular and his school was in the position of having to turn away students as the number rapidly increased.[67] On a visit to the mountain tribes north of Saigon, journalist Honda Katsuichi returned to one village and, on hearing music coming from a kite, 'immediately assumed that some Japanese transistor radio had been introduced even to this remote village, and was lashed to the frame of the kite'.[68] Only the Japanese people continued to ignore their country's economic involvement in the economies of East and Southeast Asia under the protection of the umbrella of American nuclear power. For Kugai the problem was that Japanese people maintained a division between the international and the national as well as the individual and the national.

By the end of the 1960s, however, for Kugai and other journalists covering the conflict in Vietnam, it was no longer justifiable to separate the Japanese people from the actions of the Japanese state. As Honda Katsuichi explained, after being mistaken for Korean when visiting the National Hospital in Vinh-Long, the people's 'look of hatred would gradually die away, but it left me with a bitter aftertaste. Considering the difference between Korea's open participation in the war, and Japan's present attitudes and policies towards Vietnam, we can no longer exonerate ourselves by saying "No we are Japanese"'.[69] The contradictions of Japan's situation were becoming clear. In the eyes of the people of Southeast Asia, the Japanese protested against their government's support of the United States in Vietnam only because it restricted their country's autonomy as a sovereign state. For them, Japan's involvement in Vietnam was a problem tied to the ANPO treaty. For the people of Southeast Asia encountered by Kugai and other journalists though, the problem was the economic dominance of Japan in the region. A dominance supported by the United States' war.

The people of the region saw the economic development of the Japanese economy into Southeast Asian markets, and it revived the memory of the wartime actions of the Japanese in Southeast Asia. In 1945, the Japanese army exported rice to Japan to prevent starvation in the homeland, while nearly 2 million people starved to death in Vietnam itself. Any Japanese citizen over the age of twenty-six or twenty-seven 'must have benefitted from this policy, indeed they were only able to eat because of it. We Japanese were able to continue living through the sacrifice of unknown numbers of Vietnamese. This is a shocking historical truth which cannot be denied.'[70] If and when the Japanese did think and protest about the inhuman actions of America in the

My Lai incident, they had to keep in mind that it was the Japanese who were there first. Vietnamese people absolved American people for the crimes their country committed under the belief that American imperialism and American people were different. In the same way, they saw Japanese fascists and Japanese people as different.

Yet Japanese people should not just nod at this in agreement, argued Kugai, because if it were not for the foreign rice in 1945 many young Japanese people would not have been alive. Ultimately, it was impossible to separate the people from the policies of their state. Kugai himself 'couldn't shake off the terrible idea that during the horrible experience of war I had eaten foreign rice'.[71] The Vietnamese had an ethnic national (*minzokuteki*) pride far stronger than that of the Japanese. 'They have a *minzokuteki* pride that is needed to become a yellow white man that far exceeds what we can imagine as Japanese'. After all, noted Kugai, the Vietnamese were opposing the most powerful military in history and winning.[72]

The Japanese people were enjoying the benefits of a consumer society which deflected their attention from the actions of the United States in Vietnam. The separation between national and international issues, and the actions and responsibilities of the individual and the state allowed the Japanese people in their everyday lives to separate the internal issue of economic growth from the external, international problems that growth was based upon. The growth of a consumer society under the shelter of the US-Japan alliance had brought about the economic superiority of Japan, but distanced the Japanese people from the struggles of the Vietnamese, and disavowed the political nature of Japanese economic influence in Southeast Asia. Nevertheless, in blaming the state and consumerism for people's lack of interest or empathy towards Vietnam, Kugai still opposed an authoritarian state to the need for introspection on the part of the Japanese people.

Okinawa is cheap!

The issue of Okinawa neatly encapsulated the ambiguities in the separation of internal and external, whether in the discussion of national and international or the nature of individual subjectivity. With the security treaty again due for renewal in 1970, the leaders of Beiheiren realized the importance of Okinawa as 'a corollary to the upcoming treaty issue', and discussion of 'the return' of Okinawa was rife in the popular media.[73] Nevertheless, the ambiguity in discussions between the US and the Japanese governments over the Island's return and the amount of time the talks were taking led some commentators to fear that the people on the mainland would soon lose all interest in the topic. Even for people living in Okinawa, the agreement on the return was not well thought of.[74] On the mainland, the discussion and debate in the media continued to efface the division between the national and the international and connected the issue to high-speed economic growth and individual subjectivity. Consumerism and Americanization were seen to have brought about depoliticization, rendering the Japanese people insensitive to the war and the plight of Okinawa.

Veteran anti-war protester and Beiheiren leader Iida Momo, writing in *Fujin Kōron* in December 1969, captured this dilemma. He claimed that the 'Golden Sixties' championed by Kennedy and celebrated at the start of the decade with the promotion of the consumer as king, were over. According to US president Nixon, the danger of a third world war was not a concern for America, Europe, South America or Africa, but Asia. Iida had studied geography in school, but he nevertheless went to check his atlas and desperately implored his readers to do the same because 'Japan is in Asia!' Moreover he asked his readers to run their finger over Japan because 'that's right, Okinawa is there'. The 'island in the middle of a military base … sinking under the weight of armaments' was not only supporting the Vietnam War but becoming home to most of the armaments in the Pacific area.[75] Yet as one high school student noted, 'in the classroom teachers don't talk about it. They don't want to be asked about it'. A Kanagawa School's head teacher banned the Okinawan Research Group from discussing anything other than tourism at the school's culture festival. Iida feared that because of the postwar education system people on the mainland were 'in danger of forgetting the simple fact on a map: that Okinawa is in Japan and Japan is in Asia'.[76]

As *Newsweek* explained in August 1965, Okinawa was 'one vast supply dump, training ground and advanced staging area for US forces in the Far East'. Every possible item in America's war arsenal was stored there 'from jungle knives to nuclear weapons …', and Kadena Air Force Base, just north of Naha, was one of the world's busiest airports, with camps, firing ranges and supply depots scattered 'the length and breadth of the island'.[77] But, beyond this strategic concern, what exactly was the significance of Okinawa? What was the Island's importance for people on the mainland? For Iida, Okinawa's importance seemed clear on the map and it was here that the contradictions and ambiguities of economic growth on the mainland became apparent. As Tobe Hideaki has noted, for Okinawa high-speed economic growth was part of a neocolonial political system, and never reached the levels of high-speed growth experienced on the mainland. What it did do was deepen 'dependence on the American military'.[78] In this context, Mark Selden has pointed out that by the late 1960s, the Okinawan economy was overwhelmingly dependent on the spending of the US military. After 1965, the value of Okinawan exports declined as inflation outpaced the increase in foreign sales while exports never climbed above a meagre 20 per cent of imports. This massive trade deficit was stemmed only by a desperate reliance on the US dollars provided by the salaries and expenditure of the military bases.[79]

The problems and consequences of the postwar settlement for Japan, Asia and America were made explicit in Okinawa where the contradictions of the rapid growth of a consumer society within the context of the postwar settlement were also becoming clear. In the terminal shop of Naha airport, whisky imported by America was extremely popular. Writing in *Fujin Kōron*, Iida admitted that, even though he didn't have an entry permit to visit Okinawa, his mouth was watering at the thought of Johnny Walker Black Label for six dollars, Red Label for two dollars, Napoleon Brandy for ten dollars and White Horse whisky for two dollars. No doubt he was just as tempted as the workers belonging to Sohyo who continually visited the island to protest for the return of Okinawa to Japan, but nevertheless took full advantage of the duty-free sales war to stock up on the three bottles of Johnny Walker, 600 Okinawan cigarettes and 400 foreign cigarettes allowed by the Japanese government.[80] For Oda Kaoru, the former head of Sohyo, this consumerist aspect of the reversion movement was a good thing. It was natural if workers wanted to drink 'Johnny Walker and Napoleon to make them feel better'. For Oda, the important thing for the trades union was to bring prosperity to the people of Okinawa, and for this it was necessary to demand a 'western level of lifestyle'.[81] Through twenty-six years of effort,

Okinawa had moved from 'being able to eat Japanese rice in the morning' to having what Oda termed a 'mainland level of lifestyle'. He believed that this would help ease the tensions between the Okinawans and the Americans on the island.

Iida placed the blame at the feet of the *Heibon Punch* national hero Matsushita Kōnosuke. His PHP (peace and happiness through prosperity) economics was no longer just an intellectual concept; it was the reality. The idea of goods available like running water had firmly taken root on the mainland and was being promoted in Okinawa. Iida called these ideas 'ANPO prosperity'. 'My-homeism', peace and well-being were the driving aims of the Japanese. An 'economic monster' had been born from the ANPO system. It was 'grotesque', but the irony of the system was overwhelming. Everyone went about clutching 'the neutral-coloured paper bags from the duty free shops', and buying headbands and sleeve ties proclaiming 'ANPO *Haiki*' (abolish ANPO).[82] For Iida though, the deeper problem with this desire of Okinawa to be like the mainland, or for Japan to be like the 'West', was the pursuit of the same ideas of development that had been sparked by the Meiji revolution of the nineteenth century. By 1969, this path of modernization and development through prosperity had been fundamentally brought into question.

Conclusion

The basis of Japan's postwar developmental trajectory may well have been democracy, but it needed to be remembered that this American democracy was 'killing Vietnamese outside and killing black people inside'. The Americans were losing morally and militarily in Vietnam, and so the goal of a Western lifestyle was nothing more than 'to be frank, peace and prosperity built upon the blood of Vietnamese people'.[83] Sadly, the Japanese only thought about ANPO in terms of their own advantage or disadvantage. Government talk about prosperity and lifestyle meant that the questions of ANPO and Okinawa were only discussed in terms of their profitability. In Iida's opinion, it all quite simply boiled down to one question: whether ANPO and Okinawa were 'as profitable as Johnny Walker Red Label'.

The discrimination and cold-hearted calculation which Iida complained about was one fundamental aspect of the developmental path of democracy that Japan's leaders had followed. Democracy, as Iida saw it, had 'western' style discrimination built into it. '[In] American democracy white women are free, black people are lynched, while Vietnamese are napalmed.'[84] Nevertheless, people in America and Japan went about their everyday lives turning a blind eye to this problem. Students and young people were ignored in Japan, and considered naive by their teachers. Young people were constantly told to 'study, study, study', and wait until university to begin thinking about such problems. The pressing question was, 'how do the supposedly mature teachers oppose the war in Vietnam?' The answer was simple: 'they grind their teeth and say "me I am a wife and I have children" just as if it has no relation to them at all'. Those wives and mothers clearly forgot that 'most of the people being killed are wives and have children'. If society put high school tests before thinking about the realities of the discrimination inherent in the system, then Iida believed it was time to rethink the relationship between mother and child.

The contradictions between everyday life, the economy, the international situation and the treatment of young people in Japan were becoming increasingly evident by the late 1960s. Okinawa clearly reflected the ambiguous situation in which the vast majority of people on the mainland found themselves benefitting from the hegemony of the neo-imperialism of the United States while opposing the war in Vietnam and taking pride in the idea of their country as a peaceful role model in Asia. Yet, allowing B52s to take off from Okinawa every day while talking about peace, happiness and anti-violence was a terrible contradiction, which for Iida held racist connotations. Japanese people and the state took the advantages offered by economic power and prosperity and conveniently ignored the fundamental injustice it was built upon. In short, the pursuit of the 'arrow of development', peace and happiness through prosperity, was 'ignorant, arrogant, negligent, and decadent'.[85]

The relentless consumerization of individual subjectivity was a corollary of rapid economic growth, but the rapid reconstruction of the nation depended on Japan's role as an ally of the United States in the Cold War. The introspection of the student protesters and the apparent lack of empathy among the general population to events in Vietnam or the situation on Okinawa were two sides of the same coin. The domestic development of the country could not be separated from the international context of postwar imperialism, while the promotion of individual freedom through consumption required a disavowal of the basis of an everyday life in which people sought the meaning of Japan and Japanese.

5

Conclusion

Being Japanese: *Nihonjinron*, consumer society and national subjectivity

By the 1980s, Ichimada Hisato's call for the transformation of Japanese working culture and Ikeda Hayato's invitation to come together as an autonomous people in the pursuit of a higher standard of living could be easily dismissed as selfish attempts to deflect responsibility for the disastrous events of the early 1940s away from the political decision makers of the time and onto the backward, feudalistic ways of the people. Likewise, the young prince Akihito's diary entry, written on the day of surrender in August 1945, noting that the Japanese could never have won the war because 'they thought only of their private interests rather than the county, and behaved selfishly', along with his view that, despite being superior to the Americans in every respect, 'as a group we are inferior to them', could appear as attempts to rationalize defeat.[1] Because, by the time Akihito ascended the throne at the end of the following decade, the rapid economic growth that had propelled the rise of Japan as number one was being explained in terms of Japanese cultural homogeneity and uniqueness. The supposed organic nature of groupism, the innate propensity for the Japanese to work together, rather than for individual, selfish ends, and the beneficial effects on culture of being a small country bereft of natural resources were incorporated into a discourse of Japaneseness (*Nihonjinron*) that became a commercial publishing phenomenon through the 1970s and into the 1980s.

Nihonjinron is a form of cultural nationalism. It puts the cultural traits of the people of Japan at the forefront of appeals to nation and sees in the everyday habits of the people the basis for belonging. The important thing is that there is a tendency to explain almost anything in cultural terms. This pervades the *Nihonjinron* and it serves to separate the Japanese from what could be considered 'universal' norms. As Kosaku Yoshino has pointed out, 'the Japanese have long perceived themselves to be on the periphery in relation to the "central" civilizations where the "universal" norm has been supposed to exist. China and the West have acted as models for Japan and it is against these that the Japanese have asserted their particularistic difference'.[2]

Of course, the idea that a backward culture had been responsible for the disaster of the early 1940s was not restricted to those who had played a role in leading the country into defeat. As shown in Chapter 2, many intellectuals took the early Meiji period to be the best guide for the future direction of Japanese nationalism. With wartime and prewar ideas discredited, some intellectuals set a democratic idea of nation in opposition to the negative, and ultimately disastrous, prewar state-centred nationalism (*kokkashugi*) based on feudal notions of loyalty. The deformity in Japan's nationalism could be traced back to the restoration, but the more democratic idea of nation harked back to the 'opening' of the country in the Meiji period. The ideas of Fukuzawa Yukichi and Meiji period 'enlightenment' thinkers were put forward as a model for Japan's future national identity. Some even going so far as to propose, as Mori Arinori had in the 1870s, to abolish the Japanese language and adopt French or English. As Ienaga Saburo has pointed out, even though Fukuzawa himself could be seen to support a state-centred style of nationalism, at the beginning of the Occupation he came to be seen as 'the father of Japanese democracy'.[3] In his apparent quest to establish a democratic nationalism in Japan, Fukuzawa was 'a thinker who was focused on demolishing the "feudal consciousness" imbued in the Japanese people and on rooting a "European civic culture" on Japanese soil'.[4] This was, of course, precisely the aim of the Occupation.

The adoption of explanations for the disaster of the 1940s, then, was usually based on the superiority of Western civilization and the backward, feudal nature of Japanese political, social and cultural life. This process of self-orientalism was eagerly embraced by many Japanese intellectuals and politicians in the immediate aftermath of defeat. The enormous popularity of Ruth Benedict's *The Chrysanthemum and the Sword* helped to drive this phenomenon. In *Bunkaron*, written in 1947, Tanikawa Tetsuzō disagreed with Akihito and the politicians. Echoing Benedict, he saw the problem as the lack of individualism and the tendency to place the nation state above the interests of the individual.[5] Yet this national self-criticism, or 'auto-orientalism', neatly tied in with the Occupation aims of democratizing and demilitarizing the country. The need to free the individual from the overpowering influence of the state was, as has been discussed, a driving aim of the intellectuals who debated and discussed the meaning of national identity and nationalism in the early 1950s. For them, the individual experience of everyday life held the key to preventing the autonomous Japanese people from being dominated by the return of an autocratic state or the communism of China or the Soviet Union.

The 1950s are often seen as a period of anti-nationalism broken by the emergence of a developmental nationalism that re-integrated the Japanese state into the discourse of nationalism and national identity. Emerging alongside modernization theory, 'developmentalist nationalism' for the most part rejected cultural uniqueness because exceptionalism was associated with wartime disaster. The difficulty facing the Japanese in light of the defeat in 1945 was in casting back for ideas of nation which could unite the people as the country was rebuilt. The usual symbols of national identity – the flag and the national anthem, for example – were tainted by association with wartime. Under General MacArthur the Occupation sought to rehabilitate these symbols, but even by the time of the Tokyo Olympics in 1964 they were still greeted with ambiguity and sometimes animosity. As seen in Chapter 4, it was in the spaces of entertainment and consumption that the flag and anthem were eventually rehabilitated, though they have never been completely accepted.

Beginning in the late 1960s, a large number of books, journal articles and newspaper columns began to appear asserting Japan's cultural uniqueness in a more positive light. With the aim of exposing the secrets of the country's rapid economic growth, Sydney Crawcour noted in 1980, 'Japanese intellectuals now attribute their country's economic success not to the effects of American-type modernisation but to the operation of unique traditional virtues of Japanese society, culture and personality'.[6] By the 1980s, the rapid economic growth of the 1950s and 1960s was regularly put down to the superior ability of the Japanese to work together, to put aside selfish ideals of personal advancement or enrichment and give their utmost for the success of national goals. This contrasted with the ideologically selfish and culturally divided 'West'.

It is important to understand that the *Nihonjinron* (theories of Japaneseness) were not simply expressions of economic power and a search for meaning in the light of rapid economic development. Nor were they a knee-jerk response to the Nixon shocks and the oil crisis of the early 1970s. Their appeal lay not only in the bankruptcy of developmentalist ideas of nation stemming from the end of rapid economic growth in the early 1970s, but also in the nature of consumer society in postwar Japan and the fundamental contradictions that underpinned it. For a state seeking to motivate and control a given population, nationalism offers a means of connecting ideological goals to wider cultural traits. Yet, through this link to culture, it also connects the political to the everyday life of the people. In this way, in the context of high-speed economic growth, cultural nationalism appeared muted during the period of structural transformation of the 1950s to become more predominant in the 1970s as Japan gained status as an economic power. The apparent disappearance of nationalism in the 1950s was actually the process of the embedding of the political and economic changes into the everyday lives of the people.

The return of economic and political confidence fostered, indeed set the stage for, the return of national, cultural self-confidence. As Laura Hein points out, this turn towards cultural nationalism in Japan happened, unlike in other places, '*before* the onset of any crisis in Japan's developmental strategy and *before* neoliberal economic policies were adopted'.[7] As Radhika Desai concludes, 'in Japan developmental nationalism, nation and the national economy were treated as identical … the discourse of Japanese uniqueness returned, brazenly reinstating pre-surrender themes as well as overturning developmentalist critiques'.[8] Yet, this was not so much a self-congratulatory discourse or a cynical attempt to disavow the political economy of the 1950s and 1960s. The emerging focus during the 1950s on consumerism as a driving force for the development of the economy and the connection of economic growth to the transformation of everyday life provides a key to understanding the shift from developmental nationalism to cultural nationalism.

From the mid-1950s, media discourse began to tie peace and democracy to an everyday life increasingly embedded within a consumer culture. As has been shown, this connection was political and ideological. It served to tie Japan into the global Cold War on the side of the free world; at the same time, it turned culture itself into a commodity. As Jean Baudrillard argued in 1970, advertising 'turns the object into an event. In fact, it constructs it as such by eliminating its objective characteristics. It constructs it as a model, a spectacular news item'.[9]

The popular media in the postwar period constructed the Japanese 'nation' as an event in this sense, and thus aided in its transformation from an objective concrete entity based on top-down, symbolic representation to an imagined community based on individual subjectivity.

The ANPO protests, the rebuilding of the cities, the coming of the Tokyo Olympics, international travel and the Shinkansen, the student movements and the Vietnam War were discussed and debated as 'spectacular news items'. This meant that the popular mass media helped to disavow the objective characteristics of Japan's postwar development by juxtaposing these issues with popular culture. By the late 1960s, the increasing intensity of the Vietnam War meant that the contradictions were becoming hard to ignore.

The subjective discovery of the nation

Nihonjinron can more easily be seen as an extension of the interconnection of ideas of nation with a broader, international focus on consumption and culture as the ultimate symbols of national identity. As Brian McVeigh has noted, 'Effective nationalism is like religion: it must offer something shared yet transcendent, abstract yet visible, mundane yet profound, reasonable-sounding yet inexpressible, and demonstrable yet not provable'.[10] In postwar (or post-imperial Japan as McVeigh puts it) 'Japan's version of economic progressivism has been inextricably bound up with the "capitalist developmental state" and the bureaucratic elite's view that economics is fundamentally a moralistic endeavour concerned with renovating the nation'.[11] In this context, McVeigh has examined the ways in which various institutions present different versions of nationalism that serve to make ideas of nation ambiguous, but, I would argue that it is precisely that ambiguity which allows for individual subjectivity to emerge in the imagining of the nation.

Michael Billig has shown how the nation insinuates itself into daily practices and habits. In this sense the nation is mundane, 'banal' in Billig's famous assertion. The flag not waved is as important as the flag waved or saluted. In this context, the national flag hanging on a public building, 'or decorating a filling station forecourt', illustrates what Billig terms a 'forgotten reminding'. 'Thousands upon thousands of such flags each day hang limply in public places.

These reminders of nationhood hardly register in the flow of daily attention, as citizens rush past on their daily business.'[12] Billig's point is important, but it needs to be expanded beyond state symbols and institutions usually understood to dictate representations of nation. National identity is about the context in which individuals make sense of their everyday experience. The present is a lived experience, while the past is constantly relied on to provide meaning and stability. The nation provides a spatial and temporal context for the everyday.

Here I follow Tim Edensor in seeing the multiple, changing and contesting meanings of popular cultural forms and practices as they contrast with a national identity that is commonly presented as coming from the top down, looking towards the common past and creating a boundary.[13] In the case of Japan in the 1950s and 1960s, the nature of the common past was, of course, highly contested, and the developmental ideas of nation outlined by Laura Hein looked more towards a common future. Nevertheless, it is useful to look to popular representations of nation in order to understand how the cultural ingredients of nation are mediated, contested and subject to change. In the period covered by this book the mediation of ideas of nation was tied up with the politics of development, the Cold War, consumer culture and everyday life. Tessa Morris-Suzuki suggests that 'identity is not a thing which individuals carry with them through life, like a scar on the soul. Instead, it is something that we make in the present moment out of an interweaving of our cultural resources, as we talk to others, listen, write, or read'.[14] This reworking in the present of both culture and individual identity is a central part of the process of identification with ideas of nation. During the period of rapid economic growth in postwar Japan the cultural resources of that present moment increased rapidly. The growth of the popular media in Japan from the late 1950s needs to be better understood in order to offer any account of the nationalisms of postwar Japan.

Marilyn Ivy has traced the way in which, during the 1970s, 'a high-level advertising executive, a powerful culture broker and image purveyor who scans the fringes of Japan's youth culture' could head up a team of advertising executives within Dentsu, the country's largest advertising company and create the 'Discover Japan' campaign to lead people to 'national-cultural and subjective discovery'.[15] This advertising campaign was one of the most important in postwar history. That it was so successful, and could appeal to young urban Japanese in the way it did, clearly demonstrates that the fundamental basis of the discourse of national identity and nationalism in postwar Japan connected national identity to individual subjectivity. This process was brought about by the growth of the popular media and the relentless consumerization of individual and national subjectivity through the 1950s and 1960s, because, in the postwar period, the unconscious 'flagging' of the nation takes place at the level of popular culture.

The nation and the national are imagined through the emergence of the print media. They are sustained, altered and contested by the development of that medium as it becomes a commodity. Taking Marshall McLuhan's point that 'the medium is the message' helps to contextualize the growth of *Nihonjinron* as a 'genre' in the 1970s.[16] Throughout the late 1950s and 1960s, media representation of ideas of nation shifted the emphasis on 'peace and democracy' to notions of 'peace and prosperity'. This process was accelerated by the shift in the mid-1950s from a production-led economy to one fuelled by consumption. Socially, politically and economically new patterns emerged which altered the everyday lives of the Japanese people. While these conditions were not unique to Japan, they helped Japanese people to integrate cultural ideas of nation into an apparently depoliticized popular culture. Just as the political economy of food had been projected onto Japanese food culture, consumer culture depoliticized the Cold War context of Japan's economic growth. As with other countries of the Free World, Japan emerged economically and politically within a universal vision of modernity closely tied to American hegemony. In Japan, within the context of the Cold War in Asia, the contradictions of this position became clear in the debates and discussions within the popular media. Yet as the media not only advertised, but also discussed and promoted new ways of living, the political nature of these contradictions was defused.

By the early 1960s, the apparent thaw in the Cold War, marked by the Soviet leader's visit to the United States in late 1959, seemed to make the renewal of the Security Treaty redundant. The ANPO issue became tied to the protection of postwar democracy, but although the treaty symbolized a subordinate client-state relationship between Japan and the United States, the increasing prospects brought by economic growth allowed debate and discussion to press ideas of nation which appeared to relate more concretely to the everyday lives of the people. In this way, the public celebration of consumerism in the popular media helped deflect attention from the political to the realm of everyday lived experience. The media helped to separate the Japanese state and its relationship to the United States from an image of 'America' which offered consumer lifestyles and leisure time to the Japanese people. The idea of the 'consumer as king' reflected the political imperatives of the Cold War, yet through the popular media these were deflected onto the opportunities and possibilities of a rapidly growing economy.

This was especially important for a magazine like *Shūkan Heibon* which was targeted at young working people living away from home and with some, if only a little, money to spend. As this book has shown, during the period of high-speed economic growth, popular magazines incorporated readers into a Cold War discourse, one which emphasized the 'freedom' of the individual. This focus on individual subjectivity in the 1950s and 1960s was intimately linked to the notion of Japan as a 'free' country in the context of the Cold War in East Asia. The Japanese media promoted the freedom of the individual to consume in the name of the recovery of the Japanese nation as a whole, and, as a result, the discourse on Japanese national identity became connected to the ways in which the lived experience of the Japanese people was transformed throughout the period from 1952 to 1972. In this context, the growth of the market for weekly magazines worked in two ways. On the one hand, the magazines emerged as consumer goods in an increasingly competitive market. To survive they needed to represent the lives of their readers, but, at the same time, they worked to create the desire for the lifestyles promised by the promotion of consumer society.

This growth in the popular media aided the consumerization of identities, national and individual, and connected this to the wider political, social and economic transformations of the period. For this reason, magazines aimed at housewives and those aimed at young people, in addition to daily newspapers and high-brow journals, reflect the broadening of the debate and the expansion of the possibilities for national subjectivity. The journals and magazines targeted different audiences, nevertheless they all participated in the creation of 'national space' during the period of high-speed economic growth, and by juxtaposing them it is possible to see the overlapping and conflicting nature of many of the ideas of nation that emerged.

All things to all people

Kevin Doak has recently refuted fears over the apparently statist nature of the nationalism espoused by Japanese prime minister Shinzo Abe. 'The first and most important thing to understand about Japanese nationalism is that there are two words for nationalism in the Japanese lexicon (and *kokkashugi* [statism] is not one of them): *minzokushugi* and *kokuminshugi*. When a person speaking or thinking in Japanese makes reference to "nationalism," he must choose which of these two terms to employ. And that choice makes a difference.'[17] For Doak, the two forms of nationalism, *minzokushugi* and *kokuminshugi*, have their own political and cultural history in modern Japan. Choosing one word over the other is to select 'explicitly or implicitly, a particular understanding of what nationalism is'.[18] Doak notes that Marxists and 'the left' remain quite strongly attached to nationalism. In his view, the left is wedded to a nationalism of 'the ethnic variety, whereas more conservative intellectuals and media outlets (e.g. Yomiuri newspaper) are more inclined toward civic nationalism'. Simply put, 'the former (*minzokushugi*) is best understood as "ethnic nationalism" and the latter (*kokuminshugi*) as "civic nationalism"'.[19] Doak acknowledges, without examining, the explicitly ideological nature of the division of the two terms. He notes that 'ethnic nationalism has been positioned as "Asian nationalism" at least since the 1955 Bandung Conference. In contrast, civic nationalism has, from its very beginning in modern Japan and throughout East Asia, been seen as the favourite of pro-Western governments, Christian minorities and intellectuals thought to be tainted by Western ways of thinking.'[20] The civic versus ethnic divide in studies of nationalism is, in Doak's opinion, an East/West split, and at the same time a fundamental aspect of any explanation of Japanese nationalism.

In response, Tessa Morris-Suzuki rightly points out that the separation into good=civic (*kokumin*) and bad=ethnic (*minzoku*) 'has been very effectively criticised by many scholars who argue that the notions of race, culture, tradition and citizenship bound up in nationalism are far too complex to be isolated and captured in this easy formula'.[21] Bernard Yack has been at the forefront of this debate, arguing that separating the political from the cultural in defining the nation is practically impossible.[22] Moreover, in Japan in the 1950s the terms *kokumin* and *minzoku* were often conflated. *Minzoku* nationalism (*minzokushugi*) itself was not considered a negative expression of nation. The good=civic and bad=ethnic distinction within theories of nationalism has to be viewed as a product of the postwar debate on the rejection of totalitarianism and exclusionist myths of national destiny. The debate brought Japanese ideas of nation into the emerging modernization discourse, which sought universal values and individual subjectivity within the Cold War battle for ideological allegiance. The notion that ideas of nation and expressions of nationalism can be either 'civic' or 'ethnic', with a clear understanding of the separation and differing genealogies of what those terms represent, has informed much of the debate over nation and nationalism, not only in Japan, but also in more general theoretical terms.

The problem lies in the origins of the separation of the two terms, ethnic and civic, as distinct ideas of nation. This division, first presented theoretically by Hans Kohn in the 1940s, was a useful way of separating state from nation, but more importantly of finding a place for a liberal tolerance within the particularistic cultural nature of various extreme nationalisms which had emerged in the 1930s. The nation, then, could exist outside the state in its ethnic and cultural embodiment.[23] At the same time, it could find its place in a liberal democracy by linking the individual as a member of the nation to the institutions and ideals of the democratic system. Sharing such ideals would take the place of, or at the very least temper, the organic relations of blood, language and culture, which had by the end of the Second World War (at the time of Kohn's writing) amply demonstrated the negative, exclusivist potential of ethnic and cultural nationalism.

Given the historical context of the mid–late 1940s, Kohn's dichotomy between 'civic' and 'ethnic' nationalism soon took on pejorative connotations. The connection of liberal democratic ideas to the concept of a 'civic nation' contrasted with the more 'backward' concepts of cultural nationalism, which were exclusivist in their promotion of blood and language. In the early Cold War era, the idea of the nation as a voluntary grouping of people, who as individuals are governed by the same laws through common consent, came to be seen as a Western model of nationalism, tied to the values of the enlightenment, and inherently good. The popularity of modernization theory after 1945 helped to deepen this pejorative distinction. As Anthony Smith put it, 'Historic territory, legal-political community, legal-political equality of members, and common civic culture and ideology; these are the components of the standard, Western model of the nation.' In the ethnic conception of nation, on the other hand, 'the place of law in the Western civic model is taken by vernacular culture, usually languages and customs'.[24] Such a conception is seen as leading to cultural exclusivism and discrimination.

As has been discussed, the idea of a 'good' modernity drove much debate about Japan after its defeat in 1945. In the postwar period, the debate over the development of Japanese nationalism certainly became tied up with a constant striving towards a good nationalism in the form of the ideal of a 'civic nation'. In his study of the history of nationalism in modern Japan, Kevin Doak makes a plea for the development of such nationalism, now apparently found in the administration of Shinzo Abe.[25] For intellectuals, this was tied up with the promotion of peace and democracy in the late 1940s and early 1950s, and subsumed into the debate over mass culture and mass society in the context of the ANPO protests.

In Japan, the 'civic nation' came to be represented, not by the democratic institutions of the state, but by the emergence of civic society which was then set in opposition to an increasingly powerful state. For postwar liberal intellectuals, the 'civic nation' had been continually denied in Japan through the actions of the autocratic state. With popular sovereignty inscribed in the postwar constitution under the term *kokumin*, and Marxist intellectuals framing the debate in terms of *minzoku*, both sides sought to distance the nation from the state. However, in postwar Japan, many such intellectuals picked up the prewar and Meiji era debates in an attempt to escape from the 'dark valley' of the immediate past and explain their own actions in the war years through the lens of an oppressive state which had left them little choice but to support the emperor system.[26] They found 'Japan' in opposition to the increasingly dominant state, much as young writers of the 1880s had emerged in search of the essence of 'Japaneseness' to counter the excessive Westernization of the Meiji government.

Examination of the growth of the popular media in the context of the emergence of consumer society shows that the 'flagging' of the nation or nationalism as argument, a daily plebiscite as Renan put it, does not only happen through advertisements, political will or elite discussion. Political and cultural ideas of nation cannot be separated from the political economy in which they emerge. National subjectivity helps us to understand the process, fundamental to the 1950s and 1960s, through which an individual's freedom from the overbearing influence of the state and opportunities to consume freely merged in discussion of nation and national identity with the freedom of the nation from subordination to Cold War imperialism. The freedom of the nation and its recovery and future economic development were premised on the freedom of the individual within the Cold War context of the promotion of consumption and consumer lifestyles. This was the postwar dilemma facing Japan once the Occupation ended in 1952.

The rise of popular culture, spurred by the rapid economic growth of the late 1950s, created a huge cultural matrix of images, ideas, spaces, things and practices that shaped the possibilities for national subjectivity. This term ('national subjectivity') better captures the apparent individual autonomy involved in thinking about the national in everyday life at a time when the individual, domestic, national and global were deeply entwined in Japan. If national identity and nationalism are constantly being re-imagined in changing local and global contexts through an ever-expanding range of resources, the consumer society of the 1950s and 1960s, as it emerged in and through the growth of the popular media, promoted the autonomous individual as the core of social, cultural and economic life and therefore the core of the postwar nation. It is in this context that the importance of everyday life becomes apparent. It is here too that the contradictions, ambiguities and dilemmas of postwar Japan are most evident.

Notes

Introduction

1 Ishihara Shintaro, 'Shinkairakushugi no Seikatsu Kakumei-"Mainichi ga Taikutsu da" to iu Nijū dai e no Panchi aru Adobaisu', *Heibon Punch*, 3 May 1965, p. 24.
2 Hani Motoko, 'Subete no Hito ga Kono Yō ni Kyōiku Sare, Sō Seikatsu Sureba, Kuni to Hito wa Kanarazu Tomu', *Fujin no Tomo*, Vol. 46, No. 2, February, 1952, pp. 25–26.
3 'Kotoshi no Kokumin Seikatsu o Kataru', *Asahi Shimbun*, 3 January 1952.
4 Eiji Oguma, *'Minshū' to 'Aikoku': Sengo no Nashonarizumu to Kōkyōsei* (Tokyo: Shinyōsha, 2002), p. 67; Carol Gluck, 'The Past in the Present', in Andrew Gordon Ed. *Postwar Japan as History* (Berkeley: University of California, 1991), p. 69.
5 'Subete no Hito ga Kono Yō', pp. 25–26.
6 Tsuru Shigeto, 'Watashitachi no Seikatsu Suijun', *Fujin Kōron*, March 1952.
7 Andrew Gordon, 'Society and Politics from Transwar through Postwar Japan', in Merle Goldman and Andrew Gordon Eds. *Historical Perspectives on East Asia* (Cambridge, MA: Harvard University Press, 2000), p. 273.
8 J. Victor Koschmann, *Revolution and Subjectivity in Postwar Japan* (Chicago: The University of Chicago Press, 1996), pp. 4–5.
9 Mariko Asano Tamanoi, *Under the Shadow of Nationalism: Politics and Poetics of Rural Japanese Women* (Honolulu: University of Hawaii Press, 1998), pp. 180–190.
10 John Dower, *Ways of Remembering, Ways of Forgetting: Japan in the Modern World* (New York: New Press, 2012).
11 Carol Gluck, 'The "End" of the Postwar: Japan at the Turn of the Millennium', *Public Culture*, Vol. 10, No. 1, 1993, p. 12.
12 Andrew Barshay, *State and Intellectual in Imperial Japan: The Public Man in Crisis* (Berkeley: University of California Press, 1988), p. 230.
13 Tim Edensor, *National Identity, Popular Culture and Everyday Life* (Oxford: Berg, 2002), p. 7. Masao Miyoshi, *Off Center: Power and Culture Relations Between Japan and the United States* (Cambridge, MA: Harvard University Press, 1991), pp. 124–125.
14 This connection is taken from Marilyn Ivy's comment that 'Japan has been made objective through discourse. Japan is as much a discursive construct as objective

referent'. See Marilyn Ivy, *Discourses of the Vanishing: Modernity, Phantasm, Japan* (Chicago: The University of Chicago Press, 1995), p. 1.

15 Robert Hoppens, *The China Problem in Postwar Japan: Japanese National Identity and Sino-Japanese Relations* (London: Bloomsbury, 2015), see pp. 4–5.

16 Michael Billig, *Banal Nationalism* (London: Sage, 1995).

17 Edensor, *National Identity*, p. 9.

18 This is the approach often taken in accounts of nationalism and national identity, best exemplified for Japan in Kevin Doak's important book, *Placing the People: A History of Nationalism in Modern Japan* (Leiden: Brill, 2007).

19 Edensor, *National Identity*, p. 17.

20 Brian McVeigh, *Nationalisms of Japan: Managing and Mystifying Identity* (Oxford: Rowman & Littlefield, 2004).

21 Shunya Yoshimi, 'Made in Japan: The Cultural Politics of "Home Electrification" in Postwar Japan', in Steffi Richter and Annette Schad-Seifert Eds. *Cultural Studies and Japan* (Leipzig: Leipzig Universitatsverlag, 2001), p. 117.

22 Benedict Anderson, *Imagined Communities: Reflections on the Origins and Spread of Nationalism* (London: Verso, 2006).

23 Sarah Frederick, *Turning Pages: Reading and Writing Women's Magazines in Interwar Japan* (Honolulu: University of Hawaii Press, 2006), pp. 99–101.

24 See Barbara Sato, *The New Japanese Woman: Modernity, Media and Women in Interwar Japan* (Durham: Duke University Press, 2003), p. 8.

25 These figures taken from *Shuppan Nenkan* can be found at www.stat.go.jp last accessed January 2013. Over the same period the number of magazines issued monthly barely changed. The increase in weekly magazines is an indication of the consumer-oriented nature of many of these new magazines. With fashion and trends changing rapidly, magazines needed to respond rapidly to the latest fads to survive in the market, and of course weekly magazines had the potential to pull in more advertising revenue. Sato Takumi notes this speeding up of media culture as one of the reasons for the end of *King*. See Takumi Sato, *Kingu no Jidai: Kokumin Taishū Zasshi no Kōkyōsei* (Tokyo: Iwanami Shoten, 2002).

26 Natsuko Furuya, 'Postwar Publishing Trends in Japan', *The Library Quarterly*, Vol. 32, No. 3, July, 1962.

27 Chieko Irie Mulhern, 'Hani Motoko: The Journalist Educator', in Chieko Irie Mulhern Ed. *Heroic with Grace: Legendary Women of Japan* (Armonk: East Gate, 1991), p. 262. Writing of the 1980s, Mulhern notes that the magazine 'has preserved its journalistic integrity … and remains a refreshing and reassuring, if somewhat didactic, source of practical wisdom in daily life' (p. 229) read by well-educated women of all ages with upper middle class status and family standing.

Sheldon Garon, *Molding Japanese Minds: The State in Everyday Life* (Princeton: Princeton University Press, 1997), p. 132.

28 Simon Partner, 'Taming the Wilderness: The Lifestyle Improvement Movement in Rural Japan, 1925–1965', *Monumenta Nipponica*, Vol. 56, No. 4, Winter, 2001, pp. 497–500.

29 Miriam Murase, *Cooperation over Conflict: The Women's Movement and the State in Postwar Japan* (London: Routledge, 2006).

30 Andrew Gordon, 'Managing the Japanese Household: The New Life Movement in Postwar Japan', *Social Politics*, Vol. 4, No. 2, 1997, p. 247.

31 Patricia L. Maclachlan, *Consumer Politics in Postwar Japan* (New York: Columbia University Press, 2002).

32 Matthew Hilton, 'Consumers and the State since the Second World War', *The Annals of the American Academy of Political and Social Science*, Vol. 6, No. 11, May, 2007, p. 67.

33 Andrew Gordon, 'Consumption, Leisure and the Middle Class in Transwar Japan', *Social Science Japan Journal*, Vol. 10, No. 1, 2007, pp. 239–266; Harry Harootunian, *Overcome by Modernity: History, Culture and Community in Interwar Japan* (Princeton: Princeton University Press, 2000).

34 Sato, *The New Japanese Woman,* pp. 45–47, p. 163. Also see Miriam Silverberg, 'The Modern Girl as Militant', in Gail Lee Bernstein Ed. *Recreating Japanese Women, 1600–1945* (Berkeley: University of California Press, 1991), pp. 51–72.

35 Lise Skov and Brian Moeran, 'Introduction: Hiding in the Light: from Oshin to Yoshimoto Banana', in Lise Skov and Brian Moeran Eds. *Women and Media Consumption in Japan* (Richmond: Curzon Press, 1995), p. 10.

36 Ivy, *Discourse of the Vanishing: Modernity, Phantasm, Japan*, pp. 34–54.

37 Skov and Moeran, 'Introduction', p. 11.

38 Jordan Sand, 'The Ambivalence of the New Breed: Nostalgic Consumerism in 1980s and 1990s Japan', in Sheldon M. Garon and Patricia L. Maclachlan Eds. *The Ambivalent Consumer: Questioning Consumption in East Asia and the West* (Ithaca: Cornell University Press, 2006), pp. 85–108.

39 Perhaps they were fortunate that the development of the Hakuhōdō Institute of Life and Living did not arrive till the early 1980s. See www.hakuhodo.jp/seikatsusha/hill/ last accessed 13 January 2014. It may be, of course, that the establishment of an institution to promote the 'philosophy of lifestyles' has produced the historical bias in the study of consumption in Japan. See John L. McCreery, *Japanese Consumer Behaviour: From Worker Bees to Wary Shoppers* (Richmond: Curzon, 2000), for an analysis of the research carried out by the institute.

40 See Martyn D. Smith, ' "A MAD Age": *Heibon Punch*, Student Protest, the Media and Consumer Society in Cold War Japan', *Japan Forum*, Vol. 28, No. 3, September, 2016.

Chapter 1

1 Andrew Gordon, 'Consumption, Leisure and the Middle Class', *Social Science Japan Journal*, Vol. 10, No. 1, 2007, pp. 8–9.
2 Yoshimi Shunya, '"Made in Japan": The Cultural Politics of "Home Electrification" in Postwar Japan', in Steffi Richter and Annette Schad-Seifert Eds. *Cultural Studies and Japan* (Leipzig: Leipziger Universitatsverlag, 2001), p. 107.
3 Louise Young, 'Marketing the Modern: Department Stores, Consumer Culture and the New Middle Class in Interwar Japan', *International Labor and Working Class History*, No. 55, Spring 1999, pp. 52–70.
4 Yoshimi, 'Made in Japan', p. 108.
5 Patricia Maclachlan, *Consumer Politics in Postwar Japan* (New York: Columbia University Press, 2002), pp. 78–83.
6 Sheldon Garon, *Moulding Japanese Minds The State in Everyday Life* (Princeton: Princeton University Press, 1997).
7 See Helen Macnaughtan, 'Building up Steam as Consumers', in Penelope Franks and Janet Hunter Eds. *The Historical Consumer: Consumption and Everyday Life in Japan, 1850–2000* (London: Palgrave Macmillan, 2012), pp. 79–104.
8 Michael Schaller, *Altered States: The United States and Japan since the Occupation* (New York: Oxford University Press, 1997), p. 49.
9 Bruce Cummings, 'Japan in the World System', in Gordon Ed. *Postwar Japan as History*, pp. 50–51.
10 Shigeru Yoshida, *The Yoshida Memoirs: The Story of Japan in Crisis* (London: Heinmann, 1961), p. 163, 282.
11 *The Productivity Program in Japan: A Program of Technical Cooperation Between Japan and the United States*, Japan Productivity Center/ The United States Operations Mission to Japan, 1960, pp. 2–3.
12 Shinozaki Takao, 'Shohi wa Bitoku no Keizai Shisō', in Oikawa Yoshinobu Ed. *Tokyo Orinpiku no Shakai Keizaishi* (Tokyo: Nikkei Hyōronsha, 2009), p. 79.
13 Andrew Gordon, *The Wages of Affluence, Labor and Management in Postwar Japan* (Cambridge MA: Harvard University Press, 1998), pp. 45–57.
14 William M. Tsutsui, *Manufacturing Ideology: Scientific Management in Twentieth Century Japan* (Princeton: University Press, 1998), pp. 134–136.

15 The Productivity Programme in Japan, 1960, p. 5.
16 Simon Partner, *Assembled in Japan: Electrical Goods and the Making of the Japanese Consumer* (Berkeley: University of California Press, 1999), p. 124; Gordon, *The Wages of Affluence*, p. 49.
17 Japan Productivity Center, 'Three Guiding Prinicples 1955', http://www.jpc-net.jp/eng/mission/principle.html last accessed 20 September 2013.
18 Partner, *Assembled in Japan*, pp. 121–136.
19 Tobata Seiichi quoted in Shinozaki, 'Shohi wa Bitoku', pp. 75–98.
20 Partner, *Assembled in Japan*, p. 145.
21 Yoshimi Shunya, 'Consuming America, Producing Japan', in Garon, and Maclachlan Eds. *The Ambivalent Consumer*, p. 79.
22 Macnaughtan, 'Building up Steam', pp. 79–104; Marilyn Ivy, 'Formations of Mass Cutlure', in Gordon Ed. *Postwar Japan as History*, pp. 239–259; Yoshimi, 'Consuming America', pp. 75–79.
23 Hasegawa Kenji, 'In Search of a Radical New Left,' *Stanford Journal of East Asian Affairs*, Vol. 3, No. 1, Spring, 2003.
24 Yoshimi, Shunya, 'Reisen Taisei to Amerika no Shōhi: Tashū Bunka ni Okeru [Sengo] no Chiseigaku', in Iwanami Kōza, Ed. *Kindai Nihon no Bunkashi 9, Reisen Tasisei to Shihon no Bunka 1955 Nen Igo* (Tokyo: Iwanami Shoten, 2002), pp. 31–54. See pp. 46–47.
25 Tanaka Akihiko, *20 Seiki no Nihon 2: Anzen Hoshō: Sengo 50 Nen no Mosaku* (Tokyo: Yomiuri Shimbunsha, 1997), p. 169.
26 Yoshimi, 'Reisen Taisei to Amerika', pp. 74–79.
27 Laura Nietzel, *Living Modern: Danchi Housing and Modern Japan* (Unpublished PhD Dissertation, Columbia University, 2003), pp. 4–5.
28 Tom Pendergast, *Creating the Modern Man: American Magazines and Consumer Culture 1900–1950* (Columbia: University of Missouri Press, 2000), p. 4.
29 Sato Takumi, 'King no Jidai: Rajioteki, Tokiteki Kokumin Zashii no dōin Taisei', in Aoki, Tamotsu et al. Eds. *Taishū Bunka to Masu Media* (Tokyo: Iwanami Shoten, 1999), p. 230.
30 Asaoka Takahiro, 'Kodō Seicho no Tōrai to Shukanshi Dokusha', in Yoshida Noriake and Okada Akiko Eds. *Zasshi Media no Bunkashi: Henbō Suru Sengo Paradaimu* (Tokyo: Morihasha, 2012), p. 132.
31 Barak Kushner and Sato Masaharu, 'Digesting Postwar Japanese Media', *Diplomatic History*, Vol. 29, No. 1, 2005, pp. 28–30.
32 Kristin L. Matthews, 'One Nation Over Coals: Cold War Nationalism and the Barbecue', *American Studies*, Vol. 50, No. ¾, Fall/Winter, 2009, pp. 12–13.
33 Lizabeth Cohen, *A Consumer's Republic: The Politics of Mass Consumption in Postwar America* (New York: First Vintage Books, 2004), p. 127.

34 Greg Castillo, 'Domesticating the Cold War: Household Consumption as Propaganda in Marshall Plan Germany', *Journal of Contemporary History*, Vol. 40, No. 2, 'Domestic Dreamworlds: Notions of Home in Post-1945 Europe' (April 2005), p. 273.
35 Gordon, 'Consumption, Leisure and the Middle Class', p. 18.
36 Oku Takenori, *Ronsō no Sengoshi 1945–1970* (Tokyo: Heibonsha, 2007), pp. 44–60; Also see John Dower, *Embracing Defeat: Japan in the Aftermath of World War II* (London: Penguin Books, 1999), especially chapter 5. See Adam Bronson, *One Hundred Million Philosophers: Science of Thought and the Culture of Democracy in Postwar Japan* (Honolulu: Hawai'i University Press, 2016).
37 Sato Takumi, *King no Jidai, Kokumin Taishū Zasshi no Kōkyōsei* (Tokyo: Iwanami Shoten, 2002), p. 426.
38 Asaoka, 'Kodō Seicho no Tōrai', p. 137.
39 Yoshida, Noriake, 'Zasshi Bunka to Sengo no Nihon Shakai', in Yoshida Nariake and Okada Akiko Eds. *Zasshi Media no Bunkashi: Henbō suru Sengo Paradaimu* (Tokyo: Moriwasha, 2012), pp. 20–23.
40 Asaoka, 'Kodō Seicho no Tōrai', p. 139.
41 Ibid., p. 135.
42 Furuya, 'Postwar Publishing Trends in Japan', p. 221.
43 Sakamoto Hiroshi, *Heibon no Jidai: 1950 Nendai no Taishū Gōraku Zasshi to Wakamono-tachi*(Kyoto: Showado, 2009), p. 2.
44 Ueda Yasuo, *Sengo Janarizumu no Kōbō Zasshi wa Miteita* (Tokyo: Suiyōsha, 2009), p. 87.
45 Sakamoto, *[Heibon] no Jidai*, p. 4.
46 Shiine Yamato, *Heibon Punch no Mishima Yukio* (Tokyo: Shinchōsha, 2007), p. 8.
47 Sakamoto, *Heibon no Jidai*, p. 209.
48 Ibid., pp. 275–277.
49 Ibid., p. 196.
50 Yoshihisa Kinameri, 'Hanayaka ni Kemute, Mawari wa Hoshi Bakari datta: Shūkan Heibon, Heibon Panchi and an an', *Shisō no Kagaku*, No. 135, December, 1990, p. 69.
51 Shimizu Tatsuo, 'Satsu dan Heibon Punch', in *Heibon Tsushin Sono Junen* (Tokyo: Heibon Shuppan Bushiki Gaisha Shoshi, 1970), p. 118.
52 Yōichi Akagi, *Heibon Panchi 1964* (Tokyo: Heibonsha Shinsho, 2004), pp. 38–40.
53 Shimizu, 'Satsu-dan Heibon Panchi', p. 128. See Smith, '"A MAD age": *Heibon Punch*, Student Protest, the Media and Consumer Society in Cold War Japan', pp. 337–359.

54 Scott O'Bryan, *The Growth Idea: Purpose and Prosperity in Postwar Japan* (Honolulu: University of Hawai'i Press, 2009), pp. 18–47.
55 Nietzel, *Living Modern: Danchi Housing and Modern Japan*, pp. 4–5.

Chapter 2

1 Gushima Kanesaburō, 'Nashonarizumu no Shiteki Tenbō', in Takehara Yoshifumi Ed. *Nashonarizumu no Seijigakuteki Kenkyū* (Tokyo: Sanichi Shobō, 1967), p. 15.
2 Adam Bronson, *One Hundred Million Philosophers: Science of Thought and the Culture of Democracy in Postwar Japan* (Honolulu: University of Hawai'I Press, 2016), pp. 48–49.
3 Eiji Takemae, *The Allied Occupation of Japan* (London: Continuum, 2003), Introduction p. xxxix.
4 Sakamoto Yoshikazu, 'Kakushin Nashonarizumu-shiki Ron,' *Chūō Kōron*, October 1960, p. 44.
5 Curtis Anderson Gayle, *Marxist History and Postwar Japanese Nationalism* (London: RoutledgeCurzon, 2003), pp. 42–43.
6 Mark E. Caprio and Yoneyuki Sugita, 'The U.S Occupation of Japan-Innovation, Continuity and Compromise,' in Mark E. Caprio and Yoneyuki Sugita Eds. *Democracy in Occupied japan: The U.S Occupation and Japanese Politics and Society* (London: Routledge, 2007), p. 1.
7 Cited in John W. Dower, 'Peace and Democracy in Two Systems: External Policy and Internal Conflict', in Andrew Gordon Ed. *Postwar Japan as History* (Berkeley: University of California, 1991), p. 3.
8 MakotoIokibe Ed. *Sensō, Senryō, Kōwa: 1941–1955* (Tokyo: Chūō Kōronsha, 2001), p. 404; Rikki Kersten, *Democracy in Postwar Japan: Maruyama Masao and the Search for Autonomy* (London: Routledge, 1994), pp. 13–48.
9 Nagatsuma Misao, 'Renzoku to Dansetsu no Sokoku, Senryō to Nashonarizumu', in Ken Yonehara and Misao Nagatsuma Eds. *Nashonarizumu no Jidai Seishin: Bakumatsu kara Reisengo Made* (Nara: Kizasu Shobō, 2009), pp. 97–100.
10 Eiji Oguma, *'Minshū' to 'Aikokju' Sengō Nihon no Nashonarizumu to Kokkyōsei* (Tokyo: Shinyōsha, 2004), pp. 65, 29–65.
11 Andrew E. Barshay, *State and Intellectual in Imperial Japan: The Public Man in Crisis* (Berkeley: University of California Press, 1988), p. 230.
12 John W. Dower, 'Peace and Democracy in Two Systems', chapter one in Andrew Gordon Ed. *Postwar Japan as History* (Berkeley: University of California Press, 1993, First edition), p. 4.
13 Nagatsuma, 'Renzoku to Dansetsu', pp. 104–105.

14 This column ran from the 1 March to the 15 October 1957 for a total of thirty-three articles.

15 'Aimai na Kotoba', *Asahi Shimbun,* 5 July 1957.

16 Andrew E. Barshay, *The Social Sciences in Modern Japan: The Marxist and Modernist Traditions* (Berkeley: University of California Press, 2007), p. 65.

17 Lenaga Saburō, 'Minkenron kara Nashonarizumu he', in *Minkenron kara Nashonarizumu he, Meiji Shiryō Kenkyū Renraku Kai* (Tokyo: Ochanomizu Shobō, 1957), pp. 13–32, p. 21. See also, Kersten, *Democracy in Postwar Japan: Maruyama Masao and the Search for Autonomy*, p. 149; Doak, *Placing the People: A History of Nationalism in Modern Japan*, pp. 25–27; Karube Tadashi, *Maruyama Masao and the Fate of Liberalism in Twentieth-Century Japan* (Tokyo: International House of Japan, 2008), p. 70; Kazuo Kawai, *Japan's American Interlude* (London: The University of Chicago Press, 1960), p. 235.

18 See Robert Hoppens, *The China Problem in Postwar Japan: Japanese National Identity and Sino-Japanese Relations* (London: Bloomsbury, 2015) for an account of the way in which nationalism was put to use by different sides in the debates over Japan's relationship with China.

19 Ann Sherif, *Japan's Cold War: Media, Literature and the Law* (New York: Columbia University Press, 2009), p. 206.

20 Nagai Yonosuke, 'The Roots of Cold War Doctrine, the Esoteric and the Exoteric', in Yonosuke Nagai and Akira Iriye Eds. *The Origins of the Cold War in Asia* (Tokyo: University of Tokyo Press, 1977), pp. 15–16.

21 'Nashonarizumu', *Asahi Shimbun*, 5 July 1957.

22 Eguchi Bokurō, 'Nihon ni Okeru Minzokuteki na Mono', *Chūō Kōron*, Vol. 67, No. 4, 1952.

23 See Gayle, *Marxist History and Postwar Japanese Nationalism*, p. 1 for an outline of these debates.

24 'Aimai na Kotoba', *Asahi Shimbun,* 5 July 1957.

25 Sebastian Conrad, *The Quest for the Lost Nation: Writing History in Germany and Japan in the American Century* (Berkeley: University of California Press, 2010), pp. 171–172.

26 Gushima, 'Nashonarizumu no Shiteki Tenbō', pp. 13–16.

27 Eguchi Bokurō, 'Nihon ni Okeru Minzokuteki na Mono', *Chūō Kōron*, Vol. 67, No. 4, 1952.

28 Ibid., p. 14.

29 Yanaihara Tadao, 'Minzoku no Kabu to Heiwa no Kabu', *Sekai*, No. 73, January 1952, pp. 8–17.

30 Ibid.

31 Yanaihara Tadao, 'Dokuritsu no Toshi no Seinen ni Utau', *Yomiuri Shimbun*, 3 January 1952.
32 Ibid.
33 Ibid.
34 Inoki Masamichi, 'Nihon no Minzokushugi no Hōkō', *Chūō Kōron*, Vol. 67, No. 4, 1952, p. 4.
35 Ibid., p. 6.
36 Ibid., p. 9.
37 Quoted in Sayuri Shimizu, *Creating People of Plenty* (Kent: The Kent State University Press, 2001), p. 14. See also Bruce Johnston, 'Japan: The Race Between Food and Population', *Journal of Farm Economics*, Vol. 31, No. 2, May 1949, pp. 276–292; Barak Kushner, *Slurp! A Social and Culinary History of Ramen-Japan's Favourite Noodle Soup* (Leiden: Global Oriental, 2012), pp. 195–197.
38 Crawford F. Sams, *'Medic': The Mission of an American Military Doctor in Occupied Japan and War-Torn Korea* (London: M.E. Sharpe, 1998), p. 66.
39 Kushner, *Slurp! A Social and Culinary History*, p. 181.
40 Katarzyna Cwiertka, *Modern Japanese Cuisine: Food, Power and National Identity* (London: Reaktion Books, 2006), p. 119.
41 Charles S. Maier, 'The World Economy and the Cold War in the Middle of the Twentieth Century', in Melvyn P. Leffler and Odd-Arne Westad Eds. *The Cambridge History of the Cold War* Vol. 1 (Cambridge: Cambridge University Press, 2010), pp. 45–46.
42 Harriet Friedmann, 'The Political Economy of Food: The Rise and Fall of the Postwar International Food Order', *American Journal of Sociology*, Vol. 88 (*Supplement: Marxist Inquiries: Studies of Labor, Class, and States*, 1982), pp. 248–286.
43 Ruth Jachertz and Alexander Nutzenadel, 'Coping with Hunger? Visions of a Global Food System, 1930–1960', *Journal of Global History*, Vol. 6, No. 01, March 2011, p. 104.
44 D. John Shaw, *World Food Security: A History Since 1945* (Basingstoke: Palgrave MacMillan), 2007, p. 49.
45 Takemae, *The Allied Occupation of Japan*, p. 79; Jerome B. Cohen, *Japan's Economy in War and Reconstruction* (Minneapolis: University of Minnesota Press, 1949), p. 498.
46 Nobuo Harada, *Washoku to Nihon Bunka: Nihon Ryori no Shakaishi* (Tokyo: Shōgakkan, 2005).
47 Michael Schaller, *Altered States: The United States and Japan Since the Occupation* (New York: Oxford University Press, 1997), p. 102.

48 *The History of US Exports of Wheat to Japan*, USDA Foreign Agricultural Service, GAIN Report, June 2009, p. 6.
49 Henry A. Baehr, Edward J. Bell, and Archie M. Camp, Market Potentialities for Wheat and Wheat Flour in the Far East, United States Department of Agriculture, Foreign Agriculture Report Volume 501950, 1950, p. 6.
50 Harriet Friedmann, 'The Political Economy of Food: The Rise and Fall of the Postwar International Food Order', *American Journal of Sociology*, Vol. 88, (Supplement: Marxist Enquiries: Studies of Labour, Class, and States), 1982, p. 265.
51 Howard F. Smith, 'Food Controls in Occupied Japan', *Agricultural History*, Vol. 23, No. 3, July 1949, p. 222.
52 Jerome B. Cohen, *Economic Problems of Free Japan* (Princeton: Princeton University, 1952), pp. 8–15. The plan was a scaled down version of an 'ambitious ten year plan' to increase the output of brown rice by 39 million koku by 1960.
53 Ibid., pp. 8–18. See table 7 for the figures.
54 Hiromitsu Kaneda, 'Changes in Food Consumption Patterns in Japan', in Kazushi Ohkawa, Bruce F. Johnston and Hiromitsu Kaneda Eds. *Agriculture and Economic Growth: Japan's Experience* (Princeton: Princeton University Press, 1970), pp. 409–410.
55 Vaclav Smil and Kazuhiko Kobayashi, *Japan's Dietary Transition and Its Impacts* (Cambridge, MA: MIT Press, 2012), p. 16; John Dower, *Embracing Defeat: Japan in the Aftermath of World War II* (London: Penguin Books, 1999), p. 91.
56 'Report of Japan's Food Situation For Herbert Hoover', 6 May 1946, *Political Reorientation of Japan: September 1945 to Septmeber 1948, Report of Government Section*, Appendix F14, p. 749.
57 Kaneda, 'Changes in Food Consumption Patterns in Japan', pp. 415–425.
58 'Kotoshi no Kokumin Seikatsu o Kataru.' *Asahi Shimbun*, 3 January 1952.
59 '1952: Watashitachi no Seikatsu wa?' *Yomiuri Shimbun*, 6 January 1952.
60 'Shokuryō Mondai wa Kaiketsu Shita ka', *Fujin no tomo*, August 1952, p. 21.
61 Ibid. As noted, rice imports were around half of pre-war levels although domestic production was back to the levels of the 1930s. See Cohen, *Economic Problems of Free Japan*, p. 15 and table seven for consumption figures.
62 'Shokuryō Mondai wa Kaiketsu Shita ka', p. 23.
63 Ibid., pp. 22–23.
64 'Kotoshi no Seikatsu wa Dō Naru Ka', *Fujin Kōron*, January 1952, pp. 126–131.
65 Laura Hein, *Reasonable Men Powerful Words: Political Culture and Expertise in Twentieth Century Japan* (Berkeley: University of California Press, 2004), p. 164.
66 'Kotoshi no Seikatsu wa Dō Naru Ka', pp. 127–128.
67 Ibid., pp. 127–128.

68 Ibid., p. 128.

69 'Kitai ni Somukanu Rikisaku "Nigai Kome,"' *Asahi Shimbun*, 18 March 1952.

70 Hazumi Tsuneo, 'Yōshun no Gaikoku Eiga,' *Fujin Gahō*, May 1952, No. 572, p. 107.

71 Emiko Ohnuki-Tierney, *Rice as Self: Japanese Identities Through Time* (Princeton: Princeton University Press, 1993).

72 'Kokumin Eiyo Chōsa: Kenkyu Dantai Sechi Shimei', *Yomiuri Shimbun*, 14 December 1945.

73 George Solt, 'Ramen and US Occupation Policy', in Eric Rathand Stephanie Assmann Eds. *Japanese Foodways Past and Present* (Chicago: University of Illinois Press, 2010), pp. 191–194.

74 Takemae, *The Allied Occupation*, p. 79.

75 Harada, *Washoku to Nihon Bunka*, p. 204.

76 Inagaki Naganori, 'Bitamin wo Chūshin Toshite Tabekata no Gorika', *Fujin no Tomo*, September 1952, p. 86.

77 Ronald P. Dore, *Shinohata: A Portrait of a Japanese Village* (New York: Pantheon Books, 1978), pp. 102–105.

78 See for example, 'Kokumin Eiyō Doko e Yuku?' *Yomiuri Shimbun*, 28 October 1939.

79 This is a rather high amount and Hiromitsu Kaneda puts the calorie percentage of rice in the diet in the period 1951–1953 at around 50 per cent. The figure Shimazu provides appears to match the figure given by Kaneda for the calorific amount of rice in the Japanese diet in the 1930s. See Kaneda, 'Changes in Food Consumption Patterns in Japan', p. 417. The first government white paper on national lifestyles (*Kokumin Seikatsu Hakusho*) from 1956 gives rice as 70 per cent of the daily amount of cereals consumed in 1951, but does not provide calorific information.

80 Shimazu Chitose, 'Nani o Dō Tabetara Yoi ka', *Fujin Gahō*, July 1952, No. 574, p. 144.

81 Ōkawa Kazushi, 'Nihonjin no Seikatsu Suijun', *Fujin Gahō*, July 1952, No. 574, p. 124.

82 Ibid.

83 Cwiertka, *Modern Japanese Cuisine*, pp. 135–136.

84 'Umareru Nihon Kenkō Kyōkai: Hikui Kokumin Eiyō Kaizen ni', *Asahi Shimbun*, 18 March 1952.

85 Ibid.

86 Christopher Aldous and Akihito Suzuki, *Reforming Public Health in Occupied Japan, 1945–1952: Alien Prescriptions?* (London: Routledge, 2012), pp. 131–139.

87 'Umareru Nihon Kenkō Kyōkai: Hikui Kokumin Eiyō Kaizen ni', *Asahi Shimbun*, 18 March 1952.

88 Ibid.

89 Ibid.

90 'Nani o Dō Tabetara Yoi ka', *Fujin Gahō*, July 1952, No. 574, p. 142.

91 'Kotoshi no Seikatsu wa Dō Naru ka', *Fujin Kōron*, January 1952, pp. 126–131.

Chapter 3

1 Guy Debord, *The Society of the Spectacle* (New York: Zone Books, 1995), p. 13.

2 George Packard, *Protest in Tokyo: The Security Treaty Crisis of 1960* (Princeton: Princeton University Press, 1966), pp. 221–251.

3 Hidaka Rokurō, *Go-gatsu Jūkyū Nichi* (Tokyo: Iwanami Shoten, 1960), p. 74.

4 Lee, Bock Yung, *The Political Character of the Japanese Press* (Seoul: Seoul National University Press, 1985), p. 144.

5 'Telegram From the Embassy in Japan to the Department of State', 8 June 1960, Foreign Relations of the United States, 1958–1960, Vol. XVIII, Japan; Korea, Document 172, http://history.state.gov/historicaldocuments/frus1958-60v18/d172 last accessed 2 October 2013.

6 See for example 'Hagachi Hisho Kyo Rainichi', *Yomiuri Shimbun*, 10 June.

7 Susan Reid, 'Cold War in the Kitchen: Gender and the De-Stalinization of Consumer Taste in the Soviet Union Under Khrushchev', *Slavic Review*, Vol. 61, No. 2, Summer, 2002, p. 212.

8 Greg Castillo, 'Domesticating the Cold War: Household Consumption as Propaganda in Marshall Plan Germany', *Journal of Contemporary History*, Vol. 40, No. 2, 'Domestic Dreamworlds: Notions of Home in Post-1945 Europe' (April 2005), p. 265.

9 Bernard Thomann, 'Labour Relations During the Years of High Growth', in Michael Lucken, Anne Bayard–Sakai, Emanuel Lozerand Eds. *Japan's Postwar* (Abingdon: Routledge, 2011).

10 Christopher Gerteis, *Gender Struggles: Wage-Earning Women and Male-Dominated Unions in Postwar Japan* (Cambridge, MA: Harvard University Press, 2009), p. 187; Partner, *Assembled in Japan: Electrical Goods and the Making of the Japanese Consumer*, pp. 193–224.

11 See also, Ivy, 'Formations of Mass Culture'.

12 Hiroshi, *[Heibon] no Jidai: 1950 nen no Taishu Goraku Zashii to Wakamonotachi*, pp. 4–12. See Kristin Ross, *Fast Cars, Clean Bodies: Decolonisation and the Reordering of French Culture* (London: MIT Press, 1995) especially chapter 3, for a discussion of the way in which magazines aided in the creation of new national imaginaries during the same period in France.

13 'Afureru Kokusai Iro', *Asahi Graph*, 6 November 1964.

14 See Ross, *Fast Cars*, and Paolo Scrivano, 'Signs of Americanisation in Italian Domestic Life: Italy's Postwar Conversion to Consumerism', *Journal of Contemporary History*, Vol. 40, No. 2, 'Domestic Dreamworlds: Notions of Home in Post-1945 Europe' (April 2005), pp. 317–340.

15 Fuji Shoichi and Oe Shinobu Eds, *Sengo Nihon no Rekishi Vol 2* (Tokyo: Aoki Shoten, 1970), p. 131; Eiji Oguma, *1968, Vol 1: Wakamonotachi no Hanran to Sono Haikei* (Tokyo: Shinyōsha, 2009), pp. 25–34.

16 William Marotti, *Money, Trains, and Guillotines: Art and Revolution in 1960s Japan* (Durham: Duke University Press, 2013), p. 139.

17 'Ippo Zutsu, Ippo Zutsu,' *Asahi Graph*, 12 October 1959.

18 'Amerika no Furuschev', *Asahi Graph*, 12 October 1959, p. 4.

19 'Gunshuku no Nami ga Yosetekita: Kuichigau Higashi to Nishi no Teian to Nihon no Tachiba,' *Shūkan Heibon*, 30 March 1960, pp. 18–19.

20 Nakamura Shōgo, 'Fu Shushō Hōbei no Seika', *Asahi Graph*, 12 October 1959.

21 'Yuki-doke no Naka no Kampa', *Mainichi Graph*, 7 February 1960.

22 Sekai no Me, Nihon no Me: 'Sensō no Fuan to Heiwa e no Kitai', *Fujin Kōron*, January 1960. The last two technological advances were on the wrong side of the ideological divide as far as Japan was concerned. The United States did not have a fully developed ICBM until the middle of 1959.

23 'Gunshuku no Nami' *Shūkan Heibon*, 30 March 1960. Indeed, in May 1960, not long before a planned summit in Paris, the Soviet Union shot down a US spy plane flying over its territory. Although the United States denied the claims the Soviet Union produced the pilot and the photos he had been taking at the time. It was this incident that led to the cancellation of Eisenhower's visit to Moscow.

24 'Sekai no Me, Nihon no Me: Sensō no Fuan to Heiwa e no Kitai', *Fujin Kōron*, January 1960.

25 'Kishi-san Futatabi Amerika e', *Shūkan Heibon*, 6 January 1960, p. 23.

26 The treaty referred to the US sphere of influence in terms of the 'Far East'. US bases in Japan could be used if events in this area necessitated. The term provoked much discussion, opposition and derision in the Diet during the debate over ANPO. See 'Kyokutō no Han-i o Tsuikyū Suru', *Asahi Jānaru*, 28 February 1960. This article gives the transcripts of the questions and answers given in the Diet with regard to the definition of the term 'Far East' in the treaty. See Usui Yoshimi, Ed. *ANPO 1960* (Tokyo: Chikuma Shobō, 1969), pp. 76–84. This edited edition provides articles from all the main journals and newspapers covering the protests and debates and discussion around the renewal.

27 'Takamaru ANPO Kaitei Soshi no Ugoki: Futatabi Chi o Nagashita Kokkai Seigan Demo', *Shūkan Heibon*, 11 May 1960, p. 23.

28 'Sekai no Me, Nihon no Me', *Fujin Kōron*, March 1960.

29 Laura Hein, 'Growth versus Success: Japan's Economic Policy in Historical Perspective', Chapter 4 in Gordon Ed. *Postwar Japan as History*, p. 114. As Hein notes, this is the argument made by Marilyn Ivy, James White, Koji Taira and Frank Upham in the same volume.

30 See Nakamura Takafusa, 'Ikeda Hayato: The Man Who Created the "Economic Era"', Chapter 9 in Akio Watanabe Ed. *The Prime Ministers of Postwar Japan, 1945–1995: Their Lives and Times* (London: Lexington Books, 2016), p. 128.

31 Nihon Keizai Kikakucho, 'Kokumin Seikatsu Hakusho', *Shōwa*, Vol. 31 (1956), p. 282.

32 Laura Nietzel, *Living Modern: Danchi Housing and Postwar Japan* (unpublished PhD Dissertation, Columbia University, 2003), p. 20. See also Ono Hiroshi, 'Sumai no Riso to Genjitsu-Kodo Seicho-ki no Tokyo', in Oikawa Ed. *Tokyo Orinpiku*, pp. 129–155.

33 Ito Masaya, *Ikeda Hayato* (Tokoy: Jiji Tsushinsha, 1985).

34 See Patricia Maclachlan, *Consumer Politics in Postwar Japan* (New York: Columbia University Press, 2002).

35 Nakamura, 'Ikeda Hayato', p. 128.

36 See Ito Masaya, *Ikeda Hayato*, pp. 143–144.

37 Mainichi Graph, 3 January 1960, p. 10.

38 Ibid.

39 Andrew Gordon, *Fabricating Consumers: The Sewing Machine in Modern Japan* (Berkeley: University of California Press, 2012), pp. 57–90, 162–165.

40 Andrew Gordon, 'From Singer to Shinpan: Consumer Credit in Modern Japan', in Garon and Maclachlan Eds. *The Ambivalent Consumer*, p. 156.

41 *Mainichi Graph*, 3–10 January 1960, pp. 10–11.

42 'Umi no Masu Rejya', *Mainichi Graph*, 3 July 1960, pp. 22–23.

43 'Seikatsu no Shinpo shugi: 14chyo en no Hima-tsubushi, Amerika', *Mainichi Graph*, 3–10 January, 1960, pp. 12–15.

44 'Heiwa no Naka de Utaitai: Wakai Hitotachi no Koe naki Koe', *Shūkan Heibon*, 29 June 1960, p. 26.

45 Ibid., pp. 24–25.

46 Ibid., p. 29.

47 Ibid., pp. 25–26.

48 Ibid., p. 25.

49 See Karen Kelsky, *Women on the Verge: Japanese Women, Western Dreams* (Durham: Duke University Press, 2001), pp. 9–17.

50 Christine Yano, 'Jet-Age Nationhood: Pan-American World Airways in Postwar Japan', in Christopher Gerteis and Timothy S. George Eds. *Japan Since 1945: Postwar to Postbubble* (London: Bloomsbury, 2013), p. 210. Also see Alisa Freedman, 'Bus Guides Tour National Landscapes', Chapter 6 in Alisa Freedman,

Laura Miller and Christine R Yano. Eds. *Modern Girls on the Go: Gender, Mobility and Labor in Japan* (Stanford: Stanford University Press, 2013).

51 'Shukyū 36,000 Yen mo Yume de wa nai to iu: Amerika ha Nihon Musume wo Sagashiteru', *Shūkan Heibon*, 20 January 1960, pp. 42–45.

52 Ibid., p. 42. She was the daughter of the then Education secretary, Matsuda Takecho, and was thus in a rather more privileged position than the majority of the magazine's readers.

53 Naoko Shibusawa, *America's Geisha Ally: Reimagining the Japanese Enemy* (Cambridge, MA: Harvard University Press, 2006), pp. 255–287.

54 Lonny E. Carlile, 'Economic Development and the Evolution of Overseas Tourism, 1964–1994', *Tourism Recreation Research*, Vol. 2, No. 1, 1996, pp. 11–18.

55 'Sekai wa Nihon Josei wo Matometeiru', *Fujin Kōron*, September 1964.

56 'Kanetaka Kaoru no Sekai no Tabi', *Shūkan Heibon*, 9 January 1964, pp. 54–59.

57 'Kaigai Ryokō no Pin kara Kiri Made', *Shūkan Heibon*, 14 May 1964, pp. 109–114.

58 'Sekai wa Nihon Josei wo Matometeiru', *Fujin Kōron*, September 1964.

59 'Jiyu-ka de Geki Zō Shita Musen Ryokō no Wakamono-tachi', *Heibon Punch*, 11 May 1964, pp. 106–109.

60 Hayashi Shūji, 'Josei Seiyō no Michi', *Fujin Kōron*, February 1964, pp. 110–119. The similarity to the emphasis on 'touching (fureau) nature and tradition' for the Japanese to 'discover themselves as Japanese' in the 'Discover Japan' campaign of the 1970s is striking. As Marilyn Ivy points out, the campaign appealed to nostalgia and a search for origins in response to their antithesis 'Americanised rationalism and materialism'. Ivy, *Discourses of the Vanishing: Modernity, Phantasm, Japan*, pp. 42–43. In the early 1960s, the emphasis was on participation in a 'global modernity' and both foreign travel and foreign lifestyles became important in the popular magazines covered in here.

61 Hayashi, 'Josei Seiyō no Michi', p. 117.

62 Ibid., p. 115.

63 Ibid. See Partner, *Assembled in Japan*, for a discussion of the prevalence of cheap labour and its effect on the nature of the consumer culture that emerged in the early 1960s.

64 Hayashi, 'Josei Seiyō no Michi', p. 113.

65 Ibid., p. 118.

66 Ibid., p. 119.

67 William Tsutsui, 'Introduction', in William Tsutsui and Michael Baskett Eds. *The East Asian Olympiads 1934–2008: Building Bodies and Nations in Japan, Korea and China* (Leiden: Global Oriental, 2011), p. 14. Also see Yoshikuni Igarashi, *Bodies of Memory: Narratives of War in Postwar Japanese Culture, 1945–1970* (Princeton: Princeton University Press, 2000), pp. 143–163.

68 'Kansei Isogu Hare Butai', *Asahi Graph*, 24 January 1964.
69 Sekiguchi Eri, 'Tokyo Orinpiku to Nihon Banpaku Hakurankai', in Oikawa Ed. *Tokyo Orinpikku*, pp. 1–38; Yoshikuni Igarashi, *Bodies of Memory*, pp. 143–163; Christian Tagsold, 'Modernity, Space and National Representation at the Tokyo Olympics 1964', *Urban History*, Vol. 37, No. 2, August 2010, pp. 289–300.
70 Ueyama Kazuo, 'Tokyo Orinpiku to Shibuya, Toyko', in Oikawa Ed. *Tokyo Orinpikku*, pp. 39–74; Tsutsui, 'Introduction', pp. 1–22.
71 Noriko Aso, 'Sumptuous Repast: The 1964 Tokyo Olympics Arts Festival', *Positions*, Vol. 10, No. 1, Spring 2002, p. 8.
72 'Afureru Kokusai Iro', *Asahi Graph*, 6 November 1964.
73 Tagsold, 'Modernity, Space and National Representation at the Tokyo Olympics 1964', p. 291.
74 'Yume no Kindai Toshi Tokyo Shin-chizu', *Shūkan Heibon*, 27 August 1964, p. 97. The airport as a transport hub and space of consumer culture echoed Osaka entrepreneur Kobayashi Ichizō's 1929 department store. Situated by the main Osaka station, it sold a similar dream to city dwellers with a family restaurant and a rooftop amusement area providing leisure activities for the entire family. See Sato, *The New Japanese Woman: Modernity, Media and Women in Interwar Japan*, p. 35.
75 'Yume no Chōtokkyū wa Itsu Hashiru!?' *Shūkan Heibon*, 23 January 1964, p. 111.
76 'Yume no Kindai', *Shūkan Heibon*, 27 August 1964, p. 97.
77 Furugaki Tetsurō, 'Olympic to Nihon Josei', *Fujin Kōron*, August 1964, pp. 62–64. Furugaki had been an ambassador to France between 1956 and 1961 although he was not a career diplomat. He also served as the head of NHK.
78 Ibid.
79 Ibid., p. 63.
80 The idea of women as the guardians of national culture and virtue is nothing unique to Japan, of course. It is an essential element of most expressions of modern nationalism. Nishikawa Nagao points out that in the rapid transformation of the Meiji period the home, where the mother dressed in traditional Japanese clothing, was a welcome shelter from the rapid changes of everyday life. See Nishikawa Nagao,'Nihongata Kokumin Kokka no Keisei', in *Bakumatsu Meijiki no Kokumin Kokka Keisei to Bunka Henyō* (Tokyo: Shinyōsha, 1995).
81 Furugaki, 'Olympic to Nihon', p. 63.
82 Fujiwara Yoshie, 'Abunai Gaijin', *Fujin Kōron*, October 1964.
83 Ibid., p. 88.
84 Ibid.
85 Ibid.
86 Ibid., p. 90.

87 Ibid.
88 Ibid.
89 'Olympic Watashi no Shimpai', *Fujin Kōron*, October 1964.
90 Ibid.
91 Paul Droubie, 'Foreign and Domestic Bodies: Sexual Anxieties and Desires at the Tokyo Olympics', in Tsutsui and Baskett Eds. *The East Asian Olympiads*, pp. 77–86.
92 'Anshin Shite Gaijin to Tsukiau', *Shūkan Heibon*, 23 April 1964, pp. 88–92.
93 See http://www.talkingstoryhawaii.com/special-issue/blue-eyes-tokyo-diary-linda-beech/; http://www.suntimes.com/news/obituaries/10520709-418/starred-in-the-i-love-lucy-of-japan.html, last accessed 31 March 2013; Jayson Makoto Chun, *A Nation of a Hundred Million Idiots: A Social History of Japanese Television 1953–1973* (London: Routledge, 2006), pp. 284–286.
94 'Anshin Shite Gaijin to Tsukiau', *Shūkan Heibon*, 23 April 1964, p. 92.
95 Ibid.
96 'Kokusai teki ni natta "Tokyo no Yoru" no abanchūru', *Heibon Punch*, 14 September 1964, pp. 40–43.
97 Ibid., p. 41.
98 As Paul Droubie points out, the media discourse most often sexualized the foreign, female, athletic body. Droubie, 'Foreign and Domestic Bodies', p. 82. Although in the pages of *Heibon Punch* it was the sexual availability of the foreign tourists which was emphasized.
99 Ibid.
100 'Jiyū-ka Jidai no Josei no Chie', *Fujin Kōron*, No. 578, July 1964, p. 118.
101 Daimon Kazuki, 'Kokkusan Hin to Hakurai Hin Dochira ga Yoi ka?', *Fujin Kōron*, No. 578, July 1964.
102 Ibid., p. 119; Gordon, *Fabricating Consumers*, pp. 151–186.
103 'Kongetsu no Shōten: Kōdo Seichō Seisaku to Kokumin Seikatsu', *Fujin Kōron*, March 1964.
104 Ibid., p. 80.
105 Guy Yasko, *Mishima Yukio Vs. Todai Zenkyōtō: The Cultural Displacement of Politics*, Working Papers in Asian/Pacific Studies, 95–02(Duke University, Durham, 1995), p. 9.

Chapter 4

1 'Okori no Supotsu', *Mainichi Graph*, 31 January 1960, pp. 8–10.
2 http://www.php.co.jp/en/think.php (Last accessed 2 May 2017); Konosuke Matsushita, *Quest for Prosperity: The Life of a Japanese Industrialist* (Tokyo: PHO Institute, 1988), pp. 333–337.

3 'Kore ga Sekai no Besuto Ten da', *Heibon Punch*, 26 August 1968, pp. 111–113.
4 See Eiji Oguma, *'Minshu' to 'Aikoku': Sengo no Nashonarizumu to Kōkyōsei* (Tokyo: Shinyōsha, 2002), p. 554.
5 Yasko, *Mishima Yukio Vs. Todai Zenkyōtō: The Cultural Displacement of Politics*, Working Papers in Asian/Pacific Studies, 95–02, pp. 9–12.
6 Ivy, *Discourses of the Vanishing: Modernity, Phantasm, Japan*, p. 241.
7 'Kore ga Sekai no Besuto Ten da', *Heibon Punch*, 26 August 1968, p. 110.
8 Baudrillard, *The Consumer Society: Myths and Structures*, p. 122.
9 See Smith, '"A MAD Age": *Heibon Punch*, Student Protest, the Media and Consumer Society in Cold War Japan'.
10 Nobumasa Tanaka, *Hinomaru, Kimigayo no Sengoshi* (Tokyo: Iwanami Shoten, 2000), p. 76.
11 'Kimigayo to Hinomaru o Anata wa Dō Omou?' *Shūkan Heibon*, 30 January 1964, p. 104.
12 Ibid., p. 105.
13 Yoshida, *The Yoshida Memoirs*, p. 174.
14 Ibid.
15 'Nihon Kokumin Shokun he: Ma Gensui Nentō Mesagi', *Yomiuri Shimbun*, 1 January 1949.
16 Christian Tagsold, 'The 1964 Tokyo Olympics as Political Games', *The Asia-Pacific Journal*, Vol. 23, No. 3, 6 June, 2009. Online source.
17 Tanaka, *Hinomaru, Kimigayo no Sengoshi*, esp. 11, pp. 7–10.
18 'Hinomaru he no Kanshin', *Asahi Shimbun*, 27 February 1950.
19 'Ima wa Kono Mama ni Dai Ni Kokka ga Atemo Yoi', *Asahi Shimbun*, 2 Febraury 1949.
20 'Shin Kokka Tsukurubeki ka', *Yomiuri Shimbun*, 23 January 1951.
21 Tanaka, *Hinomaru, Kimigayo no Sengoshi*, pp. 63–92.
22 'Mina de Kangaeyō: Kimigayo', *Asahi Shimbun*, 14 June 1964.
23 'Kimigayo to Hinomaru o Anata wa Dō Omou?' *Shūkan Heibon*, 30 January 1964, p. 104, 107.
24 Tanaka, *Hinomaru, Kimigayo no Sengoshi*, p. 75.
25 'Kimigayo to Hinomaru o Anata wa Dō Omou?' *Shūkan Heibon*, 30 January 1964, p. 104, 107.
26 Ibid.
27 Ibid.
28 Ibid., pp. 106–107.
29 Paul Droubie, 'Phoenix Arisen: Japan as Peaceful Internationalist at the 1964 Tokyo Summer Olympics', *The International Journal of the History of Sport*, Vol. 28, No. 16, November 2011, p. 309.

30 'Hinomaru o Miru to Kōfun Shichau', *Heibon Punch*, 21 June 1971, p. 38.

31 Ibid.

32 '11.17: Haneda', *Heibon Punch*, 1 December 1969, p. 30.

33 Thomas Havens, *Fire Across the Sea: The Vietnam War and Japan, 1965–1975* (Princeton: Princeton University Press, 1987), p. 137.

34 Lawrence W. Beer, 'Japan 1969: "My Homeism" and Political Struggle', *Asian Survey*, Vol. 10, No. 1, January 1970, p. 47.

35 'Zoom up: Tokushū', *Heibon Punch*, 4 November 1968, p. 42.

36 Havens, *Fire Across the Sea*, pp. 169–170.

37 Fuse Toyomasa, 'Student Radicalism in Japan: A "Cultural Revolution"?' *Comparative Education Review*, Vol. 13, No. 3, October 1969, p. 325.

38 Zengakuren is the abbreviation for the All-Japan Federation of Student Self-Government Associations formed in 1947. Mainly communist in orientation the federation has been riven by splits and infighting since at least the late 1950s. According to Tsurumi Kazuko writing in 1970, 'the Dictionary of the Student Movement, published in July I969, listed about 40 anti-Communist Party sects and factions, and one affiliated to the Communist Party'. See Tsurumi Kazuko, 'Some Comments on the Japanese Student Movement in the Sixties', *Journal of Contemporary History*, Vol. 5, No. 1, Generations in Conflict (1970). Also see Shimbori Michiya, 'Zengakuren: A Japanese Case Study of a Student Political Movement', *Sociology of Education*, Vol. 37, No. 3 (Spring, 1964) for a sociological examination of the make-up of the student groups in mid-1960s Japan and an attempt to account for their growing power.

39 Havens, *Fire Across the Sea*, p. 136.

40 Ann Sherif, 'The Aesthetics of Speed and the Illogicality of Politics: Ishihara Shintaro's Literary Debut', *Japan Forum*, Vol. 17, No. 2, 2005, p. 187.

41 'Henshū Techō', *Yomiuri Shimbun*, 15 January 1960.

42 Rikki Kersten, 'The Intellectual Culture of Postwar Japan and the 1968–69 University of Tokyo Struggles: Repositioning the Self in Postwar Thought', *Social Science Japan Journal*, Vol. 12, No. 2, 2009, pp. 235–237.

43 'Shashin de Miru', *Yomiuri Shimbun*, 25 December 1967.

44 Yasko, 'Mishima Yukio Vs. Todai Zenkyoto', p. 7.

45 Oguma, *1968*, Vol. 1, pp. 39–60, 67.

46 'Gebaruto Kōkōsei', *Heibon Punch*, 14 April 1969, p. 49.

47 Kersten, 'The Intellectual Culture', p. 235.

48 Jurgen Habermas, *Toward a Rational Society: Student Protest, Science and Politics* (Boston: Beacon Press, 1971), p. 32.

49 For example, 'Naze Watashi wa Kodō Suru no ka', April, 1968, Vol. 53, No. 4, pp. 96–101; 'Tokyo Daigaku no Seishun', June 1968, Vol. 53, No. 6, pp. 132–135; 'Bari

ha Yureteita', July 1968, Vol. 53, No. 7, pp. 100–105; 'Zengakuren Iinchō wa ko Kangaetiru', August 1968, Vol. 53, No. 8, pp. 134–141; 'Gakusei wa Naze Tatakau no ka', January 1969, Vol. 54, No. 1, pp. 100–143; 'Watashi ni tote Daigauku Tōso to wa nani ka', July 1969, Vol. 54, No. 7, pp. 96–101; 'Kōkkōsei ga Ima Kangaetiru Koto', December 1969, Vol. 53, No. 12, pp. 88–93; 'Bakuhatsu Suru Kōkōsei pawa', December 1969, Vol. 54, No. 12, pp. 152–157.

50 Shimada Kazuko, 'Naze Watashi wa Kodō Suru no ka', *Fujin Kōron*, April 1968, Vol. 53, No. 4, p. 99.

51 'Barikedo wo Koete', *Fujin Kōron*, January 1969, Vol. 54, No. 1, pp. 100–101, 106–107.

52 Sakuta Keiichi, 'Gakusei wa Bōsō ni Arazu', *Fujin Kōron*, January 1968, p. 92.

53 Ibid., p. 95.

54 Ibid.

55 Ibid., p. 97.

56 Kugai Saburō, 'Nihonjin wa Kiiroi Hakujin Nano ka', *Asahi Graph*, 2 February 1970, p. 24.

57 Ibid.

58 Masaya Shiraishi, *Japanese Relations with Vietnam: 1951–1987* (Ithaca: Cornell University Press, 1990), pp. 27–28.

59 Mark T. Berger, *The Battle for Asia: From Decolonisation to Globalisation* (London: RoutledgeCurzon, 2002), p. 229.

60 Shiraishi, *Japanese Realtions*, pp. 30–31.

61 Ibid.

62 This was the line of thinking that drove the peace movement (*Beiheiren*) to ally itself with the U.S. civil rights movement.

63 Kugai, 'Nihonjin wa Kiiroi Hakujin Nano ka', p. 25.

64 In his novel *Into a Black Sun* (1968), Kaiko Takeshi has the main character make the same criticism of the majority of Japanese journalists covering the war.

65 Kugai, 'Nihonjin wa Kiiroi Hakujin Nano ka', p. 26.

66 Ibid.

67 'Nihongo Juku Kei Kyū-heishi', *Asahi Graph*, 16 July 1971.

68 Katsuichi Honda, *Vietnam War: A Report Through Asian Eyes* (Tokyo: Miraisha, 1972), p. 89. Honda was mistaken and the sound was produced by a bow attached to the top of the kite.

69 Honda, *Vietnam War*, p. 149. South Korea sent 320,000 troops to Vietnam, more as a percentage of the population, than any other country. They had a fearsome reputation, and at the time of Honda's visit to the hospital in 1967 the number of Korean soldiers was reaching its peak of 50,000.

70 Kugai, 'Nihonjin wa Kiiroi Hakujin Nano ka', p. 26.

71 Ibid., p. 26.

72 Ibid.
73 Havens, *Fire Across the Sea*, pp. 173–176.
74 Nakajima Takuma, *Kodō Seichō to Okinawa Henkan* (Tokyo: Yoshikawa Tōbunkan, 2012), p. 272.
75 Iida Momo, 'Bōsō Suru Mōretsu Nippon', *Fujin Kōron*, December 1969, p. 137.
76 Ibid., p. 137.
77 Mark Selden, 'Okinawa and American Security Imperialism', in *Remaking Asia: Essays on the American Uses of Power* (New York: Pantheon Books, 1974).
78 Tobe Hideaki, 'Okinawa Senryō kara mita Nihon no Kodō Seichō', in Wada Haruki et al. Eds. *Higashi Ajia Kingendai Tsushi*, Vol. 8 (Tokyo: Iwanami Shoten, 2011), p. 254.
79 Selden, 'Okinawa and American Security', p. 289.
80 Iida, 'Bōsō Suru Mōretsu Nippon', p. 138.
81 Ibid.
82 Ibid.
83 Ibid., p. 139.
84 Ibid., p. 141.
85 Ibid.

Chapter 5

1 Herbert Bix, *Hirohito and the Making of Modern Japan* (New York: Harper Collins, 2001), pp. 534–535.
2 Kosaku Yoshino, *Cultural Nationalism in Contemporary Japan: A Sociological Enquiry* (London: Routledge, 1992), pp. 11–12.
3 Lenaga, 'Minkenron kara Nashonarizumu he'.
4 Kersten, *Democracy in Postwar Japan*, p. 149; Doak, *Placing the People*, pp. 25–27; Tadashi, *Maruyama Masao and the Fate of Liberalism in Twentieth-Century Japan*, p. 70; Kawai, *Japan's American Interlude*, p. 235.
5 See Harumi Befu, *Hegemony of Homogeneity: An Anthropological Analysis of Nihonjinron* (Melbourne: Trans Pacific Press, 2001), p. 137.
6 Quoted in Yoshino, *Cultural Nationalism in Contemporary Japan*, p. 189.
7 Laura Hein, 'The Cultural Career of the Japanese Economy', italics in the original.
8 Radhika Desai, 'Introduction: Nationalisms and Their Understandings in Historical Perspective', *Third World Quarterly*, Vol. 29, No. 3, 2008, esp. 397, pp. 397–428; 'Conclusion: From Developmental to Cultural Nationalisms', *Third World Quarterly*, Vol. 29, No. 3, esp. 649, p. 665, pp. 647–670.
9 Baudrillard, *The Consumer Society*, p. 126.

10 McVeigh, *Nationalisms of Japan*, p. 35.
11 Ibid., p. 16.
12 Billig, *Banal Nationalism*, esp. 38, pp. 39–43.
13 Edensor, *National Identity, Popular Culture and Everyday Life*, p. 17.
14 Tessa Morris-Suzuki, *Re-inventing Japan: Time, Space, Nation* (London: M.E. Sharpe, 1998), p. 208.
15 Ivy, *Discourses of the Vanishing*, pp. 35–36.
16 Marshall McLuhan, *Understanding Media: The Extensions of Man* (Cambridge, MA: MIT Press, 1994). See Kosaku, *Cultural Nationalism in Contemporary Japan* and Befu, *Hegemony of Homogeneity* for an examination of the writers and consumers of this discourse. Also see Peter N. Dale, *The Myth of Japanese Uniqueness* (London: Routledge, 1986) for a refutation of the arguments.
17 See Kevin M. Doak, 'Japan Chair Platform: Shinzo Abe's Civic Nationalism', Center for Strategic and International Studies, 15 May 2013, http://csis.org/publication/japan-chair-platform-shinzo-abes-civic-nationalism (Last accessed 1 May 2017).
18 See Doak, *Placing the People* for the outline of the development of these terms. The quote is taken from page 2. In the book Doak also covers state, society and emperor to analyse the history of nationalism.
19 Doak, 'Japan Chair Platform'.
20 Ibid.
21 Tessa Morris-Suzuki, 'The Re-branding of Abe Nationalism: Global Perspectives on Japan', *The Asia-Pacific Journal*, Vol. 11, No. 28, Series No. 1, 15 July 2013.
22 Bernard Yack, 'The Myth of the Civic Nation', *Critical Review: A Journal of Politics and Society*, Vol. 10, No. 2, 1997, Special Issue: Nationalism. Also see 'Popular Sovereignty and Nationalism', *Political Theory*, Vol. 29, No. 4, August 2001.
23 Curtis Anderson Gayle has outlined the way the idea of an ethnic nation could separate the Japanese nation from the state by examining the Marxist discourse of the immediate postwar period. See Curtis Anderson Gayle, *Marxist History and Postwar Japanese Nationalism* (London: Routledge Curzon, 2002). Kuzio Taras has examined the distinction in relation to Kohn's work in 'The Myth of the Civic State: A Critical Survey of Hans Kohn's Framework for Understanding Nationalism', *Ethnic and Racial Studies*, Vol. 25. No. 1, January 2002.
24 Anthony Smith, *National Identity* (London: Penguin, 1991), pp. 19–20.
25 See Doak, *Placing the People.*
26 Victor Koschmann, 'The Debate on Subjectivity in Post-war Japan: Foundations of Modernism as a Political Critique', *Pacific Affairs*, Vol. 4, No. 54, Winter, 1981–1982).

Bibliography

Primary sources

Newspapers

Asahi Shimbun 朝日新聞
Yomiuri Shimbun 読売新聞

Periodicals

Asahi Graph 朝日グラフ
Asahi Journal 朝日ジャナル
Chūō Kōron 中央公論
Fujin Gahō 婦人画報
Fujin no Tomo 婦人の友
Fujin Kōron 婦人公論
Heibon Punch 平凡パンチ
Mainichi Graph 毎日グラフ
Sekai 世界
Shisō 思想
Shūkan Heibon 週刊平凡

Articles and collected volumes

Beer, Lawrence W, 'Japan 1969: "My Homeism" and Political Struggle', *Asian Survey*, Vol. 10, No. 1, January, 1970.

Brown, Delmer, *Nationalism in Japan: an Introductory Historical Analysis*, Berkeley: University of California Press, 1955.

Boudreau, Frank G, 'Nutrition in War and Peace', *The Millbank Memorial Fund Quarterly*, Vol. 25, No. 3, July, 1947.

Cohen, Jerome B, 'Japan: Reform Vs. Recovery', *Far Eastern Survey*, Vol. 17, No. 12, 23 June, 1948.

Cohen, Jerome B, *Japan's Economy in War and Reconstruction*, Minneapolis: University of Minnesota Press, 1949.

Cohen, Jerome B, *Economic Problems of Free Japan*, Princeton: Princeton University, 1952.

Dore, Ronald P, 'Japan's Place in the World', *The World Today*, Vol. 22, No. 7, July, 1966.

Eguchi, Bokurō Ed. *Sengo Nihonshi*, Vol. 2, 1961, Vol. 4, 1963, Tokyo: Rekishi-gaku Kenkyū-kai.

Fitzgerald, C.P, 'East Asia After Bandung', *Far Eastern Survey*, Vol. 24, No. 8, August, 1955.

Furuya, Natsuko, 'Postwar Publishing Trends in Japan', *The Library Quarterly*, Vol. 32, No. 3, July, 1962.

Fuse, Toyomasa, 'Student Radicalism in Japan: A "Cultural Revolution"?' *Comparative Education Review*, Vol. 13, No. 3, October, 1969.

Hidaka, Rokurō, *1960-nen 5-Gatsu 16 Nichi*, Tokyo: Iwanami Shoten, 1960.

Honda, Katsuichi, *Vietnam War: A Report Through Asian Eyes*, Tokyo: Mirai-Sha, 1972.

Kurzman, Dan, *Kishi and Japan: The Search for the Sun*, New York: Ivan Obolensky, 1960.

Meijishi Kenkyū RenrakuKai, *Minkenron kara Nashonarizumu he*, Tokyo: Ochanomizu Shobō, 1957.

Nixon, Richard M, 'Asia after Viet Nam', *Foreign Affairs*, Vol. 46, No. 1, October, 1967.

Shimbori, Michiya, 'Zengakuren: A Japanese Case Study of a Student Political Movement', *Sociology of Education*, Vol. 37, No. 3, Spring, 1964.

Smith, Howard F, 'Food Controls in Occupied Japan', *Agricultural History*, Vol. 23, No. 3, July, 1949.

Takehara, Yoshifumi Ed. *Nashonarizumu no Seiji-gaku teki Kenkyū*, Tokyo: San'ichi Shobō,1967.

Tsurumi, Kazuko, 'Some Comments on the Japanese Student Movement in the Sixties', *Journal of Contemporary History*, Vol. 5, No. 1, Generations in Conflict, 1970.

X, 'The Sources of Soviet Conduct', *Foreign Affairs*, July, 1947.

Usui, Yoshimi Ed. *ANPO 1960*, Tokyo: Chikuma Shobō, 1969.

Web sources

Centre for International Studies, Newsletter, 15 May 2013, https://www.csis.org/analysis/japan-chair-platform-shinzo-abes-civic-nationalism

www.hakuhodo.jp/seikatsusha/hill/
http://history.state.gov/historicaldocuments/frus1958-60v18/d172
www.jpc-net.jp/eng/mission/principle.html
www.mofa.gov.jp
www.mtholyoke.edu/acad/intrel/nsc-68/nsc68-1.htm
www.ndl.go.jp/constitution/e/shiryo/03/076a_e/076a_etx.html
http://nsarchive.chadwyck.com/home.do
www.olympic.org/tokyo-1964-summer-olympics
www.stat.go.jp
www.suntimes.com/news/obituaries/10520709-418/starred-in-the-i-love-lucy-of-japan.html
www.talkingstoryhawaii.com/special-issue/blue-eyes-tokyo-diary-linda-beech/

Secondary sources

Aldous, Christopher and Suzuki, Akihito, *Reforming Public Health in Occupied Japan, 1945–1952: Alien Prescriptions?* London: Routledge, 2012.

Ampiah, Kweku, *The Political and Moral Imperatives of the Bandung Conference of 1955*, Folkestone: Global Oriental, 2007.

Anderson, Benedict, *Imagined Communities: Reflections on the Origins and Spread of Nationalism*, London: Verso, 2006.

Ando, Takemasa, *Japan's New Left Movements: Legacies for Civil Society*, Abingdon: Routledge, 2013.

Arima, Tetsuo, *CIA to Sengo Nihon*, Tokyo: Heibonsha Shinsho, 2010.

Arima, Tetsuo, *Nihon Terebi to CIA: Hakutsu sareta 'Shōriki Fiaru'*, Tokyo: Shinchosa, 2006.

Ariyama, Teruo and Takeyama, Akiko, *Mediashi wo Manabu Hito no Tame ni*, Kyoto: Sekai Shisōsha, 2004.

Ariyama, Teruo and Tsuganesawa, Toshihiro, *Gendai Media wo Manabu Hito no Tame ni*, Kyoto: Sekai Shisōsha, 1995.

Aso, Noriko, 'Sumptuous Repast: The 1964 Tokyo Olympics Arts Festival', *Positions* 10:1, Spring 2002.

Avenell, Simon Andrew, *Making Japanese Citizens: Civil Society and the Mythology of the Shimin in Postwar Japan*, Berkeley: University of California Press, 2010.

Barshay, Andrew E, *The Social Sciences in Modern Japan: The Marxian and Modernist Traditions*, Berkeley: University of California Press, 2004.

Barshay, Andrew E, *State and Intellectual in Imperial Japan: The Public Man in Crisis*, Berkeley: University of California Press, 1988.

Baudrillard, Jean, *The Consumer Society: Myths and Structures*, London: Sage, 2003.

Befu, Harumi, *Hegemony of Homogeneity: An Anthropological Analysis of Nihonjinron*, Melbourne: Trans Pacific Press, 2001.

Berger, Mark T, *The Battle for Asia: From Decolonisation to Globalisation*, London: RoutledgeCurzon, 2003.

Billig, Michael, *Banal Nationalism*, London: Sage, 1995.

Borden, William S, *The Pacific Alliance: United States Foreign Economic Policy and Japanese Trade Recovery, 1947–1955*, Madison: The University of Wisconsin Press, 1984.

Caprio, Mark E. and Yoneyuki, Sugita, Eds. *Democracy in Occupied Japan: The US Occupation and Japanese Politics and Society*, London: Routledge, 2007.

Carlile, Lonny E, *Divisions of Labor: Globality, Ideology and War in the Shaping of the Japanese Labor Movement*, Honolulu: University of Hawai'i Press, 2005.

Carlile, Lonny E, 'Economic Development and the Evolution of Overseas Tourism, 1964–1994', *Tourism Recreation Research*, Vol. 2, No. 1, 1996.

Castillo, Greg, 'Domesticating the Cold War: Household Consumption as Propaganda in Marshall Plan Germany', *Journal of Contemporary History*, Vol. 40, No. 2, Domestic Dreamworlds: Notions of Home in Post-1945 Europe, April, 2005.

Chun, Jayson Makoto, *A Nation of a Hundred Million Idiots? A Social History of Japanese Television, 1953–1973*, London: Routledge, 2006.

Cohen, Lizabeth, *A Consumer Republic: The Politics of Mass Consumption in Postwar America*, New York: First Vintage Books, 2004.

Conrad, Sebastian, *The Quest for the Lost Nation: Writing History in Germany and Japan in the American Century*, Berkeley: University of California Press, 2010.

Cullather, Nick, 'The Foreign Policy of the Calorie', *The American Historical Review*, Vol. 112, No. 2, April, 2007.

Cummings, Bruce, 'Japan in the World System', in Gordon, Andrew, Ed. *Postwar Japan as History*, Berkeley: University of California, 1993.

Cwiertka, Katarzyna, Ed. *Food and War in mid-Twentieth Century East Asia*, Farnham: Ashgate, 2013.

Cwiertka, Katarzyna, *Cuisine, Colonialism and Cold War: Food in Twentieth Century Korea*, London: Reaktion Books, 2012.

Cwiertka, Katarzyna, *Modern Japanese Cuisine: Food, Power and National Identity*, London: Reaktion Books, 2006.

Cwiertka, Katarzyna, 'Popularising a Wartime Diet in Wartime and Postwar Japan', *Asian Anthropology*, Vol.1, No. 1, 2002.

Dale, Peter N, *The Myth of Japanese Uniqueness*, London: Routledge, 1995.

Desai, Radhika, 'Introduction: Nationalisms and Their Understandings in Historical Perspective', *Third World Quarterly*, Vol. 29, No. 3, 2008, pp. 397–428.

Desai, Radhika, 'Conclusion: From Developmental to Cultural Nationalisms', *Third World Quarterly*, Vol. 29, No. 3, pp. 647–670.

Doak, Kevin M, *Placing the People: A History of Nationalism in Modern Japan*, Leiden: Brill, 2007.

Doak, Kevin M, 'Japan Chair Platform: Shinzo Abe's Civic Nationalism', Center for Strategic and International Studies, 15 May 2013, https://www.csis.org/analysis/japan-chair-platform-shinzo-abes-civic-nationalism (Last accessed 3 November 2017)

Dore, Ronald P, *Shinohata: A Portrait of a Japanese Village*, New York: Pantheon Books, 1978.

Dower, John, *Ways of Forgetting and Remembering: Japan in the Modern World*, New York: New Press, 2012.

Dower, John, *Embracing Defeat: Japan in the Aftermath of World War II*, London: Penguin Books, 1999.

Dower, John, *Empire and Aftermath: Yoshida Shigeru and the Japanese Experience 1878–1954*, Cambridge, MA: Harvard University Press, 1988.

Dower, John, *War Without Mercy: Race and Power in the Pacific War*, New York: Pantheon Books, 1986.

Dower, John, Ed. *Origins of the Modern Japanese State: Selected Writings of E.H. Norman*, New York: Pantheon Books, 1975.

Droubie, Paul, 'Phoenix Arisen: Japan as Peaceful Internationalist at the 1964 Tokyo Summer Olympics', *The International Journal of the History of Sport*, Vol. 28, No. 16, November, 2011.

Edensor, Tim, *National Identity, Popular Culture and Everyday Life*, Oxford: Berg, 2002.

Franks, Penelope and Hunter, Janet, Eds. *The Historical Consumer: Consumption and Everyday Life in Japan, 1850–2000*, London: Palgrave Macmillan, 2012.

Franks, Penelope, 'Consuming Rice: Food, 'Traditional' Products and the History of Consumption in Japan', *Japan Forum*, Vol. 19, No. 2, 2007.

Frederick, Sarah, *Turning Pages: Reading and Writing Women's Magazines in Interwar Japan*, Honolulu: University of Hawaii Press, 2006.

Freedman, Alisa, Laura, Miller and Christine R., Yano, Eds. *Modern Girls on the Go: Gender, Mobility and Labor in Japan*, Stanford: Stanford University Press, 2013.

Friedmann, Harriet, 'The Political Economy of Food: The Rise and Fall of the Postwar International Food Order', *American Journal of Sociology*, Vol. 88, Supplement: Marxist Enquiries: Studies of Labour, Class, and States, 1982, pp. S248–286.

Fukuzawa, Yukichi, *An Outline of a Theory of Civilisation*, Tokyo: Keio University Press, 2008.

Garon, Sheldon M, *The State and Labor in Modern Japan*, Berkeley: University of California Press, 1987.

Garon, Sheldon M, *Molding Japanese Minds: The State in Everyday Life*, Princeton: Princeton University Press, 1997.

Garon, Sheldon M. and Maclachlan, Patricia L, Eds. *The Ambivalent Consumer: Questioning Consumption in East Asia and the West*, Ithaca: Cornell University Press, 2006.

Gayle, Curtis Anderson, *Marxist History and Postwar Japanese Nationalism*, London: RoutledgeCurzon, 2003.

Gellner, Ernest, *Nations and Nationalism*, London: Blackwell, 1983.

Gerteis, Christopher, *Gender Struggles: Wage-Earning Women and Male-Dominated Unions in Postwar Japan*, Cambridge, MA: Harvard University Press, 2009.

Christopher, Gerteis and George, Timothy, Eds. *Japan Since 1945: From Postwar to Post-Bubble*, London: Bloomsbury, 2013.

Gitlin, Todd, *The Sixties: Years of Hope, Days of Rage*, New York: Bantam Books, 1987.

Gitlin, Todd, *The Whole World Is Watching: Mass Media in the Making and Unmaking of the New Left*, Berkeley: University of California Press, 2003.

Gluck, Carol, 'The "End" of the Postwar: Japan at the Turn of the Millennium', *Public Culture*, Vol. 10, No. 1, 1993, pp. 1–23.

Gluck, Carol *Japan's Modern Myths*, Princeton: Princeton University Press, 1985.

Gluck, Carol 'The People in History: Recent Trends in Japanese Historiography', *The Journal of Asian Studies*, Vol. 38, No. 1, November, 1978.

Gordon, Andrew, *Fabricating Consumers: The Sewing Machine in Modern Japan*, Berkeley: University of California Press, 2012.

Gordon, Andrew, 'Consumption, Leisure and the Middle Class in Transwar Japan', *Social Science Japan Journal*, Vol. 10, No. 1, 2007.

Gordon, Andrew, 'Consumption, Leisure and the Middle Class in Transwar Japan', in *The Wages of Affluence: Labour and Management in Postwar Japan*, Cambridge, MA: Harvard University Press, 1998.

Gordon, Andrew, Ed. *Postwar Japan as History*, Berkeley: University of California, 1993.

Gratzer, Walter, *Terrors of the Table: The Curious History of Nutrition*, Oxford: Oxford University Press, 2005.

Griffiths, Owen, 'Need, Greed and Protest in Japan's Black Market, 1938–1949', *Journal of Social History*, Vol. 35, No. 4, Summer, 2002.

Habermas, Jurgen, *Towards a Rational Society: Student Protest, Science and Politics*, Boston: Beacon Press, 1970.

Hamuro, Masato, *Gendai Nihon no Nashonarizumu*, Tokyo: Kobushi Shobō, 1983.

Harada, Nobuo, *Washoku to Nihon Bunka: Nihon Ryori no Shakaishi*, Tokyo: Shōgakkan, 2005.

Harootunian, Harry, *Overcome by Modernity: History, Culture, and Community in Interwar Japan*, Princeton: Princeton University Press, 2000.

Kenji, Hasegawa, 'In Search of a Radical New Left,' *Stanford Journal of East Asian Affairs*, Vol. 3, No. 1, Spring, 2003.

Hasegawa, Yuichi, Ed. *Nihon Gaikō no Identiti*, Tokyo: Nansōsha, 2004.

Havens, Thomas R. H, *Fire Across the Sea: The Vietnam War and Japan, 1965–1975*, Princeton: Princeton University Press, 1987.

Hein, Laura,*Fuelling Growth: The Energy Revolution and Economic Growth in Postwar Japan* Cambridge, MA: Harvard University Press, 1990.

Hein, Laura, 'In Search of Peace and Democracy: Japanese Economic Debate in Political Context', *The Journal of Asian Studies*, Vol. 53, No. 3, August, 1994.

Hein, Laura, *Reasonable Men Powerful Words: Political Culture and Expertise in Twentieth-Century Japan*, Berkeley: University of California Press, 2004.

Hein, Laura, 'The Cultural Career of the Japanese Economy: Developmental and Cultural Nationalisms in Historical Perspective', *Third World Quarterly*, Vol. 29, No. 3, 2008.

Hilton, Matthew, 'Consumers and the State since the Second World War', *The Annals of the American Academy of Political and Social Science*, Vol. 6, No. 11, May, 2007.

Hoppens, Robert, *The China Problem in Postwar Japan: Japanese National Identity and Sino-Japanese Relations*, London: Bloomsbury, 2015.

Hotta, Eri, *Pan-Asianism and Japan's War: 1931–1945*, New York: Palgrave MacMillan, 2007.

Hutchinson, J. and Smith, A.D, Eds. *Nationalism*, Oxford: Oxford University Press, 1994.

Saburō, Ienaga, 'Minkenron kara Nashonarizumu he', in *Minkenron kara Nashonarizumu he, Meiji Shiryō Kenkyū Renraku Kai*, Tokyo: Ochanomizu Shobō, 1957.

Igarashi, Yoshikuni, *Bodies of Memory: Narratives of War in Postwar Japanese Culture, 1945–1970*, Princeton: Princeton University Press, 2000.

Iokibe, Makoto, Ed. *The Diplomatic History of Postwar Japan*, Abingdon: Routledge, 2011.

Iokibe, Makoto, Ed. *Sensō, Senryō, Kōwa: 1941–1955*, Tokyo: Chūō Kōronsha, 2001.

Iokibe, Makoto, *Sensō, Senryō, Kōwa: 1955–1970*, Tokyo: Chūō Kōronsha, 2001.

Iokibe, M, Rose, C, Tomaru, J and Weste, J., Eds. *Japanese Diplomacy in the 1950s*, London: Routledge, 2008.

Iriye, Akira, *Power and Culture: The Japanese-American War, 1941–1945*, Cambridge, MA: Harvard University Press, 1981.

Iriye, Akira and Cohen, Warren I, Eds. *The United States and Japan in the Postwar World*, Lexington: University of Kentucky, 1989.

Ivy, Marilyn, *Discourses of the Vanishing: Modernity, Phantasm, Japan*, Chicago: The University of Chicago Press, 1995.

Jachertz, Ruth and Nutzenadel, Alexander, 'Coping With Hunger? Visions of a Global Food System, 1930–1960', *Journal of Global History*, Vol. 6, No. 1, March, 2011.

Johnson, Chalmers, *MITI and the Japanese Miracle: The Growth of Industrial Policy, 1925–1975*, Stanford: Stanford University Press, 1982.

Kaiko, Takeshi, *Into a Black Sun*, Tokyo: Kodansha International, 1980.

Karube, Tadashi, *Maruyama Masao and the Fate of Liberalism in Twentieth-Century Japan*, Tokyo: International House of Japan, 2008.

Kawai, Kazuo, *Japan's American Interlude*, London: The University of Chicago Press, 1960.

Kelman, Peter, *Protesting the National Identity: The Cultures of Protest in 1960s Japan*, PhD dissertation, University of Sydney, 2001.

Kelsky, Karen, *Women on the Verge: Japanese Women, Western Dreams*, Durham: Duke University Press, 2001.

Kersten, Rikki, *Democracy in Postwar Japan: Maruyama Masao and the Search for Autonomy*, London: Routledge, 1996.

Kersten, Rikki 'The Intellectual Culture of Postwar Japan and the 1968–69 University of Tokyo Struggles: Repositioning the Self in Postwar Thought', *Social Science Japan Journal*, Vol. 12, No. 2, 2009.

Kohn, Hans, *The Idea of Nationalism: A Study in Its Origins and Background*, New York: MacMillan, 1944.

Koschmann, Victor, 'The Debate on Subjectivity in Post-War Japan: Foundations of Modernism as a Political Critique', *Pacific Affairs*, Vol. 4, No. 54, Winter, 1981–1982.

Koschmann, Victor, *Revolution and Subjectivity in Postwar Japan*, Chicago: The University of Chicago Press, 1996.

Krauss, Ellis S, *Japanese Radicals Revisited: Student Protest in Postwar Japan*, University of California Press, Berkeley, 1974.

Kushner, Barak, *Slurp! A Social and Culinary History of Ramen-Japan's Favourite Noodle Soup*, Leiden: Global Oriental, 2012.

Kuzio, Taras, 'The Myth of the Civic State: A critical Survey of Hans Kohn's Framework for Understanding Nationalism', *Ethnic and Racial Studies*, Vol. 25, No. 1, January, 2002.

Lasko, Guy, *Mishima Yukio Vs. Todai Zenkyoto: The Cultural Displacement of Politics*, Working Papers in Asian/Pacific Studies 95–02, Durham: Duke University, 1995.

Lebra, Joyce C, Ed. *Japan's Greater East Asia Co-Prosperity Sphere in World War II: Selected Readings and Documents*, London: Oxford University Press, 1975.

Lee, Bock Yung, *The Political Character of the Japanese Press*, Seoul: Seoul National University Press, 1985.

Leffler, Melvyn P. and Westad, Odd-Arne, Eds. *The Cambridge History of the Cold War*, Vol. 1, Cambridge: Cambridge University Press, 2010.

Macdougall, Terry Edward, 'Yoshida Shigeru and the Japanese Transition to Liberal Democracy', *International Political Science Review*, Vol. 9, No. 1, Visionary Realism and Political Leadership, January, 1988.

Maclachlan, Patricia L, *Consumer Politics in Postwar Japan*, New York: Columbia University Press, 2002.

Macnaughtan, Helen, 'Building up Steam as Consumers', in Franks, Penelope and Hunter, Janet, Eds. *The Historical Consumer: Consumption and Everyday Life in Japan, 1850–2000*, London: Palgrave Macmillan, 2012.

Marotti, William, 'Japan 1968: The Performance of Violence and the Theatre of Protest', *The American Historical Review*, Vol. 114, No. 1, February, 2009.

Marotti, William, *Money, Trains, and Guillotines: Art and Revolution in 1960s Japan*, Durham: Duke University Press, 2013.

Maruyama, Masao, *Thought and Behaviour in Modern Japanese Politics*, London: Oxford University Press, 1969.

Matsushita, Konosuke, *Quest for Prosperity: The Life of a Japanese Industrialist*, Tokyo: PHP Institute, 1988.

McCreery, John L. *Japanese Consumer Behaviour: From Worker Bees to Wary Shoppers*, Richmond: Curzon, 2000.

McLuhan, Marshall, *Understanding Media: The Extensions of Man*, Cambridge, MA: MIT Press, 1994.

McVeigh, Brian, *Nationalisms of Japan: Managing and Mystifying Identity*, Oxford: Rowman & Littlefield, 2004.

Miyagi, Taizo, 'Post-War Japan and Asianism', *Asia-Pacific Review*, Vol. 13, No. 2, 2006.

Miyoshi, Masao, *Off Center: Power and Culture Relations Between Japan and the United States*, Cambridge, MA: Harvard University Press, 1991.

Morris, Ivan, *Nationalism and the Right Wing in Japan: A Study of Postwar Trends*, London: Oxford University Press, 1960.

Morris-Suzuki, Tessa, *A history of Japanese Economic Thought*, London: Routledge, 1989.

Morris-Suzuki, Tessa, *Re-inventing Japan: Time, Space, Nation*, London: M.E. Sharpe, 1998.

Morris-Suzuki, Tessa, 'The Rebranding of Abe Nationalism: Global Perspectives on Japan', *The Asia-Pacific Journal*, Vol. 11, No. 28, Series No. 1, 15 July, 2013.

Mulhern, Chieko Irie, Ed. *Heroic with Grace: Legendary Women of Japan*, Armonk: East Gate, 1991.

Nagai, Yonnosuke and Iriye, Akira, *The Origins of the Cold War in Asia*, Tokyo: University of Tokyo Press, 1977.

Takuma, Nakajima, *Kodō Seichō to Okinawa Henkan*, Tokyo: Yoshikawa Tōbunkan, 2012.

Nakamura, Masanori, *Sengoshi*, Tokyo: Iwanami Shoten, 2005.

Nakamura, Takafusa, *The Postwar Japanese Economy Its Development and Structure*, Tokyo, University of Tokyo Press, 1981.

Nara, Hiroshi, Ed. *Yoshida Shigeru: Last Meiji Man*, Lanham: Rowman and Littlefield, 2007.

Nietzel, Laura, *Living Modern: Danchi Housing and Modern Japan*, PhD Dissertation, Columbia University, 2003.

Nishikawa, Nagao, *Bakumatsu Meijiki no Kokumin Kokka Keisei to Bunka Henyō*, Tokyo: Shinyōsha, 1995.

O'Bryan, Scott, *The Growth Idea: Purpose and Prosperity in Postwar Japan*, University of Hawai'i Press, Honolulu, 2009.

Oguma, Eiji, *'Minshu' to 'Aikoku': Sengo no Nashonarizumu to Kōkyōsei*, Tokyo: Shinyōsha, 2002.

Oguma, Eiji, A Genealogy of 'Japanese' Self-images, Melbourne: Trans Pacific Press, 2002.

Oguma, Eiji, *1968*, Vol. 1 & 2, Tokyo: Shinyōsha, 2009.

Ohnuki-Tierney, Emiko, *Rice as Self: Japanese Identities Through Time*, Princeton: Princeton University Press, 1993.

Oi, Koichi, *Rokujunen Anpo: Media ni Arawareta Image Tosō*, Tokyo: Keishobo, 2010.

Oikawa, Yoshinobu, Ed. *Tokyo Orinpiku no Shakai Keizaishi*, Tokyo: Nikkei Hyōronsha, 2009.

Ōkawa, K., Johnston, B. F. and Kaneda, H, Eds. *Agriculture and Economic Growth: Japan's Experience*, Princeton: Princeton University Press, 1969.

Olson, Lawrence, *Ambivalent Moderns: Portraits of Japanese Cultural Identity*, Savage: Bowman & Littlefield, 1992.

Olson, Lawrence, *Japan in Postwar Asia*, London: Pall Mall Press, 1970.

Otsuka, Shinichi, Ed. *Taishū Bunka to Media, Kindai Taishū Bunka ron 7*, Tokyo: Iwanami Shoten, 1999.

Packard, George, *Protest in Tokyo: The Security Treaty Crisis of 1960*, Princeton: Princeton University Press, 1966.

Park, Sang-mi, 'The Paradox of Postcolonial Korean Nationalism: State-Sponsored Cultural Policy in South Korea, 1965–Present', *Journal of Korean Studies*, Vol. 15, No. 1, Fall, 2010.

Partner, Simon, *Assembled in Japan: Electrical Goods and the Making of the Japanese Consumer*, Berkeley: University of California Press, 1999.

Partner, Simon, 'Taming the Wilderness: The Lifestyle Improvement Movement in Rural Japan 1925–1965', *Monumenta Nipponica*, Vol. 56, No. 4, Winter, 2001.

Pharr, Susan J. and Kraus, Ellis S, Eds. *Media and Politics in Japan*, Honolulu, University of Hawai'i Press, 1996.

Pyle, Kenneth J, *The New Generation in Meiji Japan: Problems of Cultural Identity, 1885–1895*, Stanford: Stanford University Press, 1969.

Rath, Eric and Assmann, Stephanie, Eds. *Japanese Foodways Past and Present*, Chicago: University of Illinois Press, 2010.

Reid, Susan, 'Cold War in the Kitchen: Gender and the De-Stalinization of Consumer Taste in the Soviet Union under Khrushchev, *Slavic Review*, Vol. 61, No. 2, Summer, 2002.

Ross, Kristin, *Fast Cars and Clean Bodies: Decolonization and the Reordering of French Culture*, Cambridge, MA: MIT Press, 1996.

Ross, Kristin, *May '68 and Its Afterlives*, Chicago: The University of Chicago Press, 2002.

Sakai, Naoki, deBarry, Brett and Toshio, Iyotani, *Deconstructing Nationality*, Ithaca: Cornell University, 2005.

Sakamoto, Hiroshi, *Heibon no Jidai: 1950 nen no Taishu Goraku Zashii to Wakamonotachi*, Tokyo: Shōwadō, 2009.

Sams, Crawford F, *"Medic" The Mission of an American Military Doctor in Occupied Japan and War-Torn Korea*, London: M.E. Sharpe, 1998.

Sato, Barbara, *The New Japanese Woman: Modernity, Media and Women in Interwar Japan*, Durham: Duke University Press, 2003.

Sato, Takumi, *Kingu no Jidai: Kokumin Taishū Zasshi no Kōkyōsei*. Tokyo: Iwanami Shoten, 2002.

Schaller, Michael, *The American Occupation of Japan: The Origins of the Cold War in Asia*, Oxford: Oxford University Press, 1985.

Schaller, Michael *Altered States: The United States and Japan since the Occupation*, New York: Oxford University Press, 1997.

Selden, Mark, Ed. *Remaking Asia: Essays on the American Uses of Power*, New York: Pantheon Books, 1974.

Seraphim, Franziska, *War Memory and Social Politics in Japan, 1945–2005*, Cambridge, MA: Harvard University Press, 2006.

John, Shaw D, *World Food Security: A History Since 1945*, Basingstoke: Palgrave MacMillan, 2007.

Sherif, Ann, 'The Aesthetics of Speed and the Illogicality of Politics: Ishihara Shintarō's Literary Debut', *Japan Forum*, Vol. 17, No. 2, 2005.

Sherif, Ann, *Japan's Cold War: Media, Literature and the Law*, New York: Columbia University Press, 2009.

Shigematsu, Setsu, 'Feminism and Media in the Late Twentieth Century: Reading the Limits of a Politics of Transgression', in Molony, Barbara and Kathleen, Uno, Eds. *Gendering Modern Japanese History*, Cambridge, MA: Harvard University Asia Center, 2005, pp. 555–589.

Shimazu, Naoko, Ed. *Nationalisms in Japan*, London: Routledge, 2006.

Shimizu, Kazuhiko, 'Reshaping the Social Memory of the Miyuki-Zoku: The Agents and Reconstruction Process Focusing on the Interaction and Roles of Van, Heibon Punch, Other Media and Audience', *Communication & Society, Bulletin of Edogawa University*, November, 2013, Edogawa University, pp. 215–235.

Shimizu, Sayuri, *Creating People of Plenty: The United States and Japan's Economic Alternatives, 1950–1960*, Kent: Kent State University Press, 2001.

Tatsuo, Shimizu, 'Satsu dan Heibon Punch', in *Heibon Tsushin Sono Junen*, Tokyo: Heibon Shuppan Bushiki Gaisha Shoshi, 1970.

Shin, Gi-Wook and Robinson, Michael, Eds. *Colonial Modernity in Korea*, Cambridge, MA: Harvard University Press, 1999.

Shinmura, Hiroshi, *Shoku to Ningen Keisei: Kyōiku toshite no Gakkō Kyūshoku*, Tokyo: Aoki Shoten, 1983.

Shiraishi, Masaya, *Japanese Relations with Vietnam: 1951–1987*, Ithaca: Cornell University Press, 1990.

Shulman, Stephen, 'Challenging the Civic/Ethnic and East/West Dichotomies in the Study of Nationalism', *Comparative Political Studies*, Vol. 35, 2002, p. 554.

Singer, Brian C. J, 'Contractual versus Cultural Nationalism: Rethinking Their Opposition', *History and Theory*, Vol. 35, No. 3, October, 1996.

Skov, Lise and Moeran, Brian, Eds. *Women and Media Consumption in Japan*, Richmond: Curzon Press, 1995.

Smil, Vaclav and Kobayashi, Kazuhiko, *Japan's Dietary Transition and Its Impacts*, Cambridge, MA: MIT Press, 2012.

Smith, Anthony D, *National Identity*, London: Penguin, 1991.

Smith, Robert J, *Kurusu: The Price of Progress in a Japanese Village 1951–1975*, Stanford: Stanford University Press, 1978.

Steele, M. William, *Alternative Narratives in Modern Japanese History*, London: RoutledgeCurzon, 2003.

Steinhoff, Patricia, 'Hijackers, Bombers and Ban Robbers: Managerial Style in the Japanese Red Army', *Journal of Asian Studies*, Vol. 48, No. 4, November, 1989.

Suzuki, Takeo, *Amerika Komugi Senryaku to Nihonjin no Shokuseikatsu*, Tokyo: Fujiwara Shoten, 2009.

Tachi, Mikiko, *The Folk Music Revival Then and Now: Politics, Commercialism and Authenticity in Folk Music Communities in the US and Japan*, PhD dissertation, Brown University, 2009.

Takemae, Eiji, *The Allied Occupation of Japan*, London: Continuum, 2003.

Tamanoi, Mariko Asano, *Under the Shadow of Nationalism: Politics and Poetics of Rural Japanese Women*, Honolulu: University of Hawaii Press, 1998.

Taga, Futoshi, 'Rethinking Japanese Masculinities: Recent Research Trends', in Mclelland, M. and Dasgupta, R, Eds. *Genders, Transgenders and Sexualities in Japan*, London: Routledge, 2005, pp. 153–167.

Akihiko, Tanaka, *20 Seiki no Nihon 2: Anzen Hoshō: Sengo 50 Nen no Mosaku*, Tokyo: Yomiuri Shimbunsha, 1997.

Tanaka, Nobumasa, *Hinomaru-Kimigayo no Sengoshi*, Tokyo: Iwanami Shoten, 2000.

Tanaka, Stefan, *Japan's Orient: Rendering Pasts into History*, Berkeley: University of California Press, 1993.

Tasgold, Christian, 'Modernity, Space and National Representation at the Tokyo Olympics 1964', *Urban History*, Vol. 37, No. 2, August, 2010.

Tasgold, Christian, 'The 1964 Tokyo Olympics as Political Games', *The Asia-Pacific Journal*, Vol. 23, No. 3, 8 June, 2009.

Tomiyama, Hidehiko, *Media Riterashi no Shakai shi*, Tokyo: Seikyusha, 2005.

Trentman, Frank, Ed. *The Making of the Consumer: Knowledge, Power and Identity in the Modern World*, Oxford: Berg, 2006.

Tsutsui, William M, *Manufacturing Ideology: Scientific Management in Twentieth Century Japan*, Princeton: Princeton University Press, 1998.

Tsutsui, William M. and Baskett, Michael, Eds. *The East Asian Olympiads 1934–2008: Building Bodies and Nations in Japan, Korea and China*, Leiden: Global Oriental, 2011.

Ueda, Yasuo, *Sengo Janarizumu no Kōbō Zashii wa Miteita*, Tokyo: Suiyōsha, 2009.

Haruki, Wada et al., Eds. *Higashi Ajia Kingendai Tsushi*, Vol. 8, Tokyo: Iwanami Shoten, 2011.

Ward, Vanessa B, 'The Spectre of the Left: Iwanami Shoten, Ideology and Publishing in Early Postwar Japan', *Japanese Studies*, Vol. 26, No. 2, 2006.

Watanabe, Akio, *The Okinawa Problem: A Chapter in Japan-U.S. Relations*, Carlton: Melbourne University Press, 1970.

Weiner, Michael, *Japan's Minorities: The Illusion of Homogeneity*, London: Routledge, 2009.

Wheeler, Donald Frederick, *The Japanese Student Movement: Value Politics, Student Politics and the Tokyo University Struggle*, PhD dissertation, Columbia University, 1974.

Whittemore, Edward P, *The Press in Japan Today a Case Study*, Columbia: University of South Carolina Press, 1961.

Yack, Bernard, 'Popular Sovereignty and Nationalism', *Political Theory*, Vol. 29, No. 4, August, 2001.

Yack, Bernard, 'The Myth of the Civic Nation', *Critical Review: A Journal of Politics and Society*, Vol. 10, No. 2, 1997, Special Issue: Nationalism.

Yamanouchi, Hisaaki, 'Mishima Yukio and His Suicide', *Modern Asian Studies*, Vol. 6, No. 1, 1972, pp. 1–16.

Yamato, Shiine, *Heibon Punch no Mishima Yukio*, Tokyo: Shinchōsha, 2007.

Yasko, Guy, *Mishima Yukio Vs. Todai Zenkyōtō: The Cultural Displacement of Politics*, Working Papers in Asian/Pacific Studies, 95–02, Durham: Duke University, 1995.

Ken, Yonehara and Misao, Nagazuma, Eds. *Nashonarizumu no Jidai Seishin: Bakumatsu kara Reisengō made*, Nara: Kizasu Shobō, 2009.

Yoshida, Noriake, 'Zasshi Bunka to Sengo no Nihon Shakai', in Yoshida, Nariake and Okada, Akiko, Eds. *Zasshi Media no Bunkashi: Henbō suru Sengo Paradaimu*. Tokyo: Moriwasha, 2012, pp. 10–38.

Shigeru, Yoshida, *The Yoshida Memoirs: The Story of Japan in Crisis*, London: Heinmann, 1961.

Yoshikawa, Hiroshi, *Kōdo Seichō: Nihon o kaeta 6000 nichi*, Tokyo: Yomiuri Shimbunsha, 1997.

Yoshimi, Shunya, *Posuto-sengō Shakai*, Tokyo: Iwanami Shinsho, 2009.

Yoshimi, Shunya, 'Reisen Taisei to Amerika no shōhi: Tashū Bunka ni Okeru [Sengo] no Chiseigaku', in *Kindai Nihon no Bunkashi 9, Reisen Tasisei to Shihon no Bunka 1955 Nen Igo*, Tokyo: Iwanami Shoten, 2002, pp. 31–54.

Yoshimi, Shunya, '"Made in Japan": The Cultural Politics of "Home Electrification" in Postwar Japan', in Richter, Steffi and Schad-Seifert, Annette, Eds. *Cultural Studies and Japan*. Leipzig: Leipziger Universitatsverlag, 2001.

Yoshimi, Shunya 'Consuming America, Producing Japan', in Garon, Sheldon M. and Maclachlan, Patricia L. Eds. *The Ambivalent Consumer: Questioning Consumption in East Asia and the West*, Ithaca: Cornell University Press, 2006.

Yoshimoto, Takaaki, *Nashionarizumu*, Tokyo: Chikuma Shobō, 1964.

Yoshino, Kosaku, *Cultural Nationalism in Contemporary Japan: A Sociological Enquiry*, London: Routledge, 1992.

Young, Louise, 'Marketing the Modern: Department Stores, Consumer Culture and the New Middle Class in Interwar Japan', *International Labor and Working Class History*, Vol. 55, Spring, 1999.

Index